Weibo Feminism

Weibo Feminism

*Expression, Activism, and Social
Media in China*

Aviva Wei Xue and Kate Rose

BLOOMSBURY ACADEMIC
LONDON • NEW YORK • OXFORD • NEW DELHI • SYDNEY

BLOOMSBURY ACADEMIC
Bloomsbury Publishing Plc
50 Bedford Square, London, WC1B 3DP, UK
1385 Broadway, New York, NY 10018, USA
29 Earlsfort Terrace, Dublin 2, Ireland

BLOOMSBURY, BLOOMSBURY ACADEMIC and the Diana logo are
trademarks of Bloomsbury Publishing Plc

First published in Great Britain 2022

A catalogue record for this book is available from the British Library.

Library of Congress Cataloging-in-Publication Data

Names: Xue, Aviva Wei, author. | Rose, Kate, author.
Title: Weibo feminism : expression, activism, and social media in China /
Aviva Wei Xue and Kate Rose.
Description: New York, NY : Bloomsbury Academic, Bloomsbury Publishing,
2022. | Includes bibliographical references and index.
Identifiers: LCCN 2021045818 (print) | LCCN 2021045819 (ebook) |
ISBN 9781350231498 (hardback) | ISBN 9781350231481 (paperback) |
ISBN 9781350231504 (eBook) | ISBN 9781350231511 (ePDF) |
ISBN 9781350231528
Subjects: LCSH: Feminism–China. | Women and socialism–China. |
Internet and women–China.
Classification: LCC HQ1767 .R65 2022 (print) | LCC HQ1767 (ebook) |
DDC 305.420951—dc23/eng/20211115
LC record available at https://lccn.loc.gov/2021045818
LC ebook record available at https://lccn.loc.gov/2021045819

ISBN: HB: 978-1-3502-3149-8
       PB: 978-1-3502-3148-1
       ePDF: 978-1-3502-3151-1
       eBook: 978-1-3502-3150-4

Typeset by RefineCatch Limited, Bungay, Suffolk
Printed and bound in Great Britain

To find out more about our authors and books visit www.bloomsbury.com
and sign up for our newsletters.

Contents

Illustrations

INTRODUCTION

Scattered Revolutions Spark the Masses

A massive and influential autonomous feminist movement in China today has been overlooked in the West. It is difficult to imagine the diverse and colorful forms of feminist activism now thriving in the restrictive political context of China. As a typical model of male-dominated politics, the Party-state system sees low female representation.[1] Political power is highly centralized, and historical narratives focus on male conquests. Currently, "national rejuvenation" is on the agenda, with decreasing tolerance of dissidents or of "universal values" of Western democracy. Surveillance, censorship, crackdowns on NGOs, and pro-natalist policies and neo-Confucian rhetoric against women's rights rise against a backdrop of severe sex-ratio imbalance due to decades of selective abortions and female infanticide. This is not a likely time for feminist opposition to thrive, and even planning to hand out stickers against sexual harassment has led to arrests.

Nonetheless, Chinese feminism today is thriving and has become a major influence on the public overall. Despite the disadvantages they face, more than half of all college graduates are women. Through success in the highly competitive college entrance examination, women balance the sex ratio in universities, despite being outnumbered by their male peers in secondary schools.[2] Today, even with increasing discrimination against women in the job market, Chinese women hold half of all professional and technical positions (positions requiring skills and professionalism rather than manual labor) – a leader globally. Chinese women overall are well-educated, professional, hard-working, and self-reliant; it is therefore not surprising that they have found ways to speak out and claim their rights. Autonomous feminism in China is also a vital voice of dissent calling for social reformation, just as the urgent appeal to liberate women drove China toward modernization from the late nineteenth century onward.

The digital age provides new opportunities for feminists to express and circulate their ideas, and Weibo has been an important gathering place for feminists since its creation in 2009. Weibo, or Sina-Weibo, literally meaning microblogs, is an online platform resembling Twitter, although Weibo blogs can be much longer than Tweets—up to 5,000 Chinese characters (words). Longer articles can be published on an affiliated system with convenient links. This enables deeper analytical essays and even research reports to circulate freely on Weibo. Weibo is China's largest online community with 224 million daily active users and 511 million monthly active users, of which 54.6 percent are female.[3] Nevertheless, Weibo is by no means an impartial platform for women's or feminist voices. Its operators and high-level executives have participated in the verbal attack against feminists repeatedly, and it is rather hard to decide whether most suspensions and blocks of feminist accounts and censors of feminist terms are initiated by Weibo or ordered by the authorities. Many female users were initially following showbiz news on Weibo as fans of stars, forming a fandom culture. But topics under discussion inevitably extend to wide social and political issues. Large numbers of female users guarantee a comparatively female-friendly cyber atmosphere for critical ideas from female perspectives.

Early Weibo feminism was influenced by Western liberalism and opposed Party-state feminism represented by the All-China Women's Federation. Modern Chinese feminism began at the end of the nineteenth century, and feminists with various political stances contributed to the Chinese nationalist and communist revolution and to social progress/modernization. With the establishment of the People's Republic of China in 1949, the All-China Women's Federation annexed all feminist organizations. Since then the Federation, as an institution led by the Party-state, has monopolized the political or social work concerning women, which is usually referred to as *funü gongzuo*, women's work, or work targeting women. With this rhetoric, women as a group are the object of the "work," which is initiated by the Party-state. Priorities of the Party-state have always taken precedence over women's concerns in the Federation's agenda. The strong Marxist ideals of the Maoist age (1949–1978) meant some real improvements in women's education and participation in social productivity and politics. These influenced women's lives and social norms profoundly. In the 1950s, China met the goal that every county-level government have at least one female leader, surpassing most developed countries at the time.[4]

However, the Federation can by no means go beyond the political yoke of male-dominated centralized communism. The definitions of feminism and of women's liberation officially belong to the Party. Feminism is not allowed as an exchange of ideas among women defining themselves but is instead a male-defined communist interpretation. In other words, women's agency is usurped in the ideological and political movement bound with them. In the controlling of and "planning" for women's bodies, the Party-state exposes its patriarchal core: Reproduction has always been hijacked by national will, whether forbidding abortion and contraception in the 1950s, the one-child policy from 1978 to 2015, or the current coerced childbirth with the latest "three-children policy." Women also need higher scores than men to access educational and professional opportunities (a kind of reverse affirmative action). Such effective control depends on the Party-state's monopoly of women's work through institutions such as the Women's Federation.

From the 1980s, as China opened to the outside world, Western liberal ideas gained popularity in China. The government discovered that, although China was considered backward economically and politically, women's social status, as shown by education and labor participation, was arguably higher than in the Western world. This was highlighted in propaganda domestically and internationally. With the Fourth World Conference on Women hosted in Beijing in 1995, programs and research centers on women's studies opened in universities and institutions, and NGOs on women's issues were established. Most were/are still linked with or under the umbrella of the Women's Federation or other institutions with governmental endorsement, while some are supported by foreign funds and follow Western liberalist ideology. These are all organized mainly by elite intellectuals.[5]

Digital mass media such as Weibo provide platforms for the public to express their opinions and confront the Party-state's monopoly on Chinese feminism. Feminist-related online talks first betrayed a prominent influence of Western liberalism.[6] Then, a sprouting feminist awareness from the masses challenged conservative social norms and encouraged sexual liberation.[7] There was sometimes opposition between feminists influenced by Western liberalism and those loyal to communism (with or without voicing support for the Party-state). From the beginning, however, a small group of autonomous feminists emerged independent of both government ideology and Western liberalism, and from this Weibo feminism grew into a massive force.[8]

In 2015, the Feminist Five, young college-educated women, were arrested for planning to hand out stickers against sexual harassment on subways.[9] Meanwhile, government media criticized public intellectuals as influenced by Western anti-China propaganda and attempted to crack down on their influence. The Western model of feminist activism, including demonstrations in public places in support of opinion leaders, is difficult in China. Because of close government surveillance and swift responses, feminists (like any other politically active group) will be removed before the public has noticed them. In addition, male supremacists not affiliated with the government would be likely to harass feminists whose personal information has been exposed. To resist misogynistic forces inside and outside the government, feminism must depart from elitism and sink into the everyday life of China, creating a distinctly Chinese and populist feminism.

In 2017, the Me Too movement spread to China from the West. For the authorities, it is another problem brought by Western culture, and they tightened censorship of "foreign enemies." The spirit behind Me Too—mutual support among women—is not Western-specific, and it actually fits into the Chinese context perfectly. Joining a growing torrent of protesters rather than confronting powerful institutions individually makes sense to ordinary Chinese people, and they are willing to take part. Many young women stood up to accuse professors or superiors, including some social celebrities, of sexual assaults. Though the authorities later attempted to dampen the heated public criticism by limiting media coverage, Me Too has been a catalyst for Chinese feminism to grow into a mainstream public movement. Some of the initial accusers have continued to evolve feminist ideas on Weibo.[10]

In the wake of Me Too, an autonomous and inclusive feminist community snowballed on Weibo, and it subsequently spread to other digital platforms such as Douban (a platform for public scoring and commenting on books, films, and other cultural products and forming chat groups) and short video platforms such as TikTok. Weibo has been the most renowned gathering place for the "notorious extreme feminists" for years, and is also a major public digital platform with hundreds of millions of users, where content from other platforms is reposted. We have coined the term "Weibo feminism" to refer to autonomous feminist expression and activism online. As in-person feminist activism is not allowed outside the government-backed Federation, and because of its widespread appeal among all sectors of

Chinese women, we consider Weibo feminism a synonym for Chinese feminism.

Voicing their opinions online as individuals, Weibo feminists vary in many viewpoints, which often leads to flaming arguments. But generally speaking, they are both independent from state-sponsored institutions such as the Women's Federation and also critical of Western liberalism. This dual independence distinguishes them from previous Chinese feminist movements. U.S. liberal feminism is no longer a lighthouse for Chinese feminists, and they are highly critical of it for ideological rather than nationalistic reasons. Weibo feminists stress women's agency; they approach issues in a female-centered way that refuses the traps of false egalitarianism, universalism, or choice. They accuse U.S. liberalism plus capitalist consumerism of encouraging women to embrace downward freedom, such as the free choice to be housewives, mutilate their bodies, sell their eggs, and work as prostitutes and surrogate mothers. They also question the alliance with an LGBTQ movement globally dominated by the interests of those born male. Alongside reassessment of U.S. feminism, Weibo feminists explore feminist movements in South Korea, Japan, and Latin America with the goal of true transnationality. Korean feminism especially, with the establishment of the Women's Party on March 8, 2020, has earned high praise and attention from Chinese feminists.

Most feminists consider China's current government hostile to women's rights and hindering their work; however, they do not view the Party-state as the ultimate or permanent enemy. The omnipresent patriarchal social and cultural mechanism is the foundation of politics. The masses, male and female, are accustomed to the exploitation of women as the ultimate solution to their personal problems. Weibo feminists are faced with a large number of women-hating male supremacist and nationalist groups similar to incels (involuntarily celibates) in the U.S., and also with numb and silent majority unconscious of a systematic problem and thus cooperative with the dominant mechanism. The aim of Weibo feminism is to subvert patriarchy as a whole rather than to target the current regime.

Weibo feminist methodology combines political ideology and personal life, realizing political aims through personal choices. It encourages women to seek success, grasp power, and gain a voice in society. Rather than sinking into the political confrontation against the authoritarian government, Weibo feminists believe the ultimate feminist action is women's striving for better lives for themselves. This might not sound very radical, but it is: They encourage women to refuse marriage, make their own reproductive decisions, grant their own surnames to any children they have ("stop creating patriarchs"), and fight for inheritance rights. They also stand in solidarity with women who speak out against violence and discrimination, and with China's minorities, giving voice to their words online.

Breaking the patriarchal myth that the patriarch/father is the creator of life, Weibo feminists consider this role as created through exploitation of women's reproductive abilities. They refer to women as the first sex. Anti-feminist men typically threaten women, while even the most extreme feminists only seek to be separated from men. This suggests, even with all the privileges granted by patriarchy, men fear and rely on women and cannot bear being deprived of access to the first sex. Without accessing women and hijacking their power, patriarchal constructions would collapse immediately. Unlike males furthering political aims through war, killing, and confrontation, as long as a considerable portion of women accomplish self-awareness of their power as the first sex, the feminist agenda might be realized without bloodshed.

This focus on radical personal liberation does not mean that Weibo feminism ignores public issues. Feminist discourse forms a counter narrative to confront everyday misogyny in mainstream media. In many cases, Weibo feminists have roused public opinion enough to successfully pressure the authorities to take action. Based on their respective areas of expertise or awareness, feminists address specific issues from organizing female hygiene products donations for frontline medical workers during the COVID-19 response to protesting against government charity the Spring Bud Project (publicized as aiding girls in poor areas but embezzling donations to help boys instead), and contacting the police to launch investigations of violent misogynistic cartoon pornography and rape videos circulating online. With the priority of achieving small victories one after another (rather than extreme ideological confrontations), feminists call their work "moving one pawn each time" (日拱一卒). Millions of women make small efforts every day and march forward steadfastly, ultimately changing the game.

Weibo feminists intentionally choose a scattered, decentralist way to strive toward their goal. In 2018, there were still several iconic feminist accounts on Weibo, each of whom published dozens of blogs every day on topics concerning women.[11] The authorities abolished their accounts repeatedly, summoned them to the local police, and they were harassed by anti-feminist males. Meanwhile, being an iconic figure invites many arguments, including from some feminists who considered their personal choices harmful to the circulation of feminist ideas. Weibo feminists then realized that having leaders is not conducive to Chinese cyber-feminism. They proposed the methodology of scattered revolutions, decentralizing the feminist community, including changing recognizable usernames and giving up accounts with tens of thousands of followers. Some bloggers, especially those who provide in-depth analysis and clarify patriarchal myths, constantly change their names. Giving up personal authority, feminists are free from personal attacks and slandering, and they can concentrate on spreading their ideas. As one of them remarked: "I transformed into a tiny drop of water and hid back into the parade." The parade is growing.

Weibo Feminism begins with the most recent important public outbreak of feminist dissent. During the COVID-19 response, the professionalism of female workers stood in sharp contrast to the information blockade, vanity, and inefficiencies in resources coordination of male-dominated politics. In addition to backing up female professionals and protesting against misogynistic government propaganda, feminists organized donation delivery to the locked-down epicenter. Afterward, the attempt of government institutions, including the Women's Federation and the Communist Youth League, to hijack feminist efforts as tools for propaganda suffered public outcry.

This book explores Weibo feminist thought and discourse, from reviving historical feminists to opposing marriage and Confucian filial doctrines. Approaching the famous one-child policy in a new, feminist way, the book places the policy within a long history of hijacking women's bodies. Feminist intersectional discussions of nationalism and socialism play an essential role for feminism in the Chinese context. Feminist cultural creations, including verbal innovations against misogynistic language, contribute to the feminist community. There are also feminist artists publicizing original pictures on Weibo, some of which we include in the relevant topics.

It's time to see the actual faces of Chinese feminists online. The slandering and attacks against feminists either describe them as privileged bourgeoisie or as emotional, uncivilized hoards with neither knowledge nor jobs. Even some research accepts these false descriptions, which we will dissect, showing that Weibo feminists come from diverse ethnical, class, cultural, and religious backgrounds, including property owners, businesswomen, doctors, researchers, teachers, legal workers, ordinary laborers, self-employed painters and writers of online novels, and students from middle school to PhD candidates. The only commonality is that they exhibit robust vitality and are representative of Chinese women: Diligent, hard-working, independent, and professional. But unlike other Chinese women, they refuse to comply with patriarchy and are unwilling to see their efforts embezzled for the construction of anti-women institutions.

1

Feminist Outbreaks in the Digital World

On February 6, 2020, Liang Yu (username @梁钰 stacey) posted on China's largest microblogging app Weibo asking whether there were places to donate feminine hygiene products to female medical staff working in the coronavirus epicenter of Hubei province. Hearing a lot about the lack of various materials, she immediately sensed that women on the frontline must also endure difficulty during their periods. By the following day, many doctors and nurses had confirmed their urgent need. As no donation channels were available, Liang initiated the Stand By Her project (姐妹战疫安心行动) to organize donations herself. With no relevant experience or examples to follow, Liang enrolled a team of 91 volunteers online (87 of whom were women) and cooperated with Lingshan Charity Foundation, an authorized charity organization, to collect public donations. To deliver the female hygiene products, which were not listed as emergency relief supplies in the locked-down regions of Hubei, Liang and her team contacted manufacturers who had storage in Hubei and found transporters (mostly volunteers) who had licenses to enter the lockdown regions. The timeline and details of this work have been closely compiled in an article posted on Weibo, authorized by Liang's team, for public reference (Chenmi 2020).

Working more than 20 hours a day, Liang led her team in an efficient and transparent way, sending materials worth more than two million yuan (over 330,000 USD) to 84,500 workers in 205 medical teams (Chenmi 2020). Liang publicized daily on her Weibo account the exact amounts of money spent and items distributed. By making every step traceable, the project leaves no excuses for government interference or anti-feminist slandering. Her successful endeavor led to Liang Yu's invitation to the 2020 Girl Up Leadership Summit sponsored by the U.N. Foundation.

In addition to the devoted work of Liang and her team, the project was able to run successfully because of feminists on Weibo, who garnered public concern through protesting against period shame and supporting the needs and contributions of women during the pandemic. In light of recurrent exposure of corruption and inefficiency in government initiatives, the public chose to trust a grassroots feminist project. Chinese feminists have used Weibo for years to voice criticism, facing censorship of posts and accounts, harassment, and persecution. The power they nonetheless accumulated in swaying public opinion found an outlet during the pandemic period.

Global responses to COVID-19 have exacerbated inequalities (Fortier 2020; Czymara et al. 2020; Morse and Anderson 2020), and Weibo feminists have highlighted China's everyday marginalization of women brought to the surface during the pandemic. The discrepancy between Chinese women's professional contributions and their powerless status in politics and society was brought to the forefront. Women make up 51.7 percent of professional and technical workers in China, surpassing their male peers. The female–male ratio in professional and technical workers ranks first in the world.[1] However, despite women "holding up half of the sky" professionally, they are oppressed and exploited under male-dominated politics and misogynistic mass culture. Only 16.8 percent of legislators, senior officials, and managers are women. The female–male ratio of births has long remained the world's lowest. As for overall gender equality, China now ranks 107th among the 156 countries listed, its worst ranking since the annual Global Gender Gap Report was first published in 2006.

The COVID-19 response stems from the long-existing tension between female professionalism and masculine hierarchal politics.

According to the National Health Commission of China, 28,000 female medical workers across China were sent to the epicenter of Wuhan, making up two-thirds of the total workforce (Ke 2020). According to U.N. Women (2020), it is even higher: "In Hubei province, China, the epicenter of the initial outbreak, more than 90 percent of the health-care workers on the frontline response to COVID-19 are women" (15). The men who control the coordination of resources failed to provide ample support to women working on the frontline, and it was brought to public attention that those in public decision-making positions (mostly men) usually neglect women's contributions and needs.

Why is such contradictory inequality found in China? Women receive education, are trained to be doctors, teachers, scholars, and technical workers, but do not gain decision-making and resource-coordinating positions. Women participate in social production, support their families, are independent and self-reliant, yet families still do not want girls. If Chinese women's power is not used to protect and empower themselves, where does their power go?

The existing political and cultural mechanism hijacks and diverts women's power for the benefit of their opponents. Currently, a massive autonomous feminist movement is breaking this cycle and restoring women's agency in women's work. Digital mass media provides unprecedented opportunities to bring feminists together. Recognizing the potential and growing success, the government is doing its best to block feminists from using this tool.

Before exploring Weibo feminist knowledge and methodology, this chapter will focus on the COVID-19 response and how the authorities have attempted to hijack women's power or erase their existence. It will also discuss how women defend their autonomy and agency, create their own counternarratives, construct political common ground based on their sex, and refuse to be tokenized.

Stand by her: Feminists Against Hijacking

The COVID-19 response was met by civil society organizations, which were very efficient compared to the government's response. Women initiated or participated in many such organizations. When the Wuhan government stopped all public transportation without any alternative measures in a city of more than 8,000 square kilometers with 11 million people, citizens in Wuhan organized a group of volunteer drivers to transport medical workers every day (China Daily 2020). A cafe run by a young woman named Tian Yazhen provided 7,850 cups of free coffee to medical workers after the lockdown began (Xie 2020). Han Hong Love Charity Foundation, established by the famous female singer Han Hong, raised money via public donations and transported medical equipment and supplies worth more than 200 million yuan.[2] Among those public self-organizing projects, Stand By Her stands out as a feminist project supporting the needs of female frontline workers when the established social and political institutions failed to address these needs.

Liang Yu highlights women's agency in the Stand By Her project. The project reinforces women's identity as citizens and professionals and resists marginalization in male-centered nationalist narratives. The movement conveys feminist ideals that appeal to public disappointment with government corruption and mismanagement. The project's slogan is "Sisters Combating the Pandemic Free from Worries,"[3] emphasizing solidarity and mutual aid. The logo depicts volunteers delivering donations to a medical team from Xinjiang. Avoiding symbols related to beauty and vulnerability, it shows women working for public welfare. Liang also replaced the dot on the character 心 (heart) with a used sanitary pad. This not only manifests the theme of the project; it is also a bold protest against period shame.

This affirmation of women's agency and ability stands in stark contrast to government rhetoric regarding the pandemic, which was "superficial at best and anti-feminist to the core" (C. Chen 2020). The hashtag "Sisters Combating the Pandemic Free from Worries" differs greatly from "Paying Respect to the Amazing Her" (致敬了不起的她) created by the government's All-China Women's Federation, "Publicizing the Most Beautiful Her" (晒晒最美的她) by the *People's Daily* and "Thank You, My Goddess" (谢谢你我的女神) by CCTV (China Central Television). "Paying respect to" is recurrent political rhetoric in China and otherizes its object "her," expelling "her" to a passive position. Other hashtags divert attention from needs of female workers to their appearance, using them as tokens.

The Stand By Her project, highlighting women's agency, conflicts with both rampant male supremacism and the official nationalist narratives online. These tend to degrade, otherize, silence, and sexualize women. From the beginning of the project, Liang was attacked by anti-feminist forces as not qualified to organize the donations, and her project was slandered as illegal fundraising. The real meaning of "not qualified" is that women are not supposed to organize and coordinate social resources outside official institutions such as the Women's Federation. They are not even supposed to get themselves hygiene supplies; they are only qualified to follow the authorities' instructions and wait patiently to be "paid respects to." The anti-feminist attackers erroneously placed their hope in the authorities to abolish the women's project.

Liang and other feminists intentionally established feminist socialist narratives, which is probably one reason the authorities are conflicted about shutting the project down. Using the hashtag "recognize female workers,"[4] many feminist posts not only request equal media exposure for female workers but also urge that the nation, which describes itself as a socialist republic, put women's needs and the equal status they deserve into the national agenda. This involves restructuring socialism with feminist agency and reframing socialist concerns as feminist concerns. Weibo feminists advocate for integration of women's current everyday realities into a reconstruction of socialism.

When calling for the addition of menstrual products into the emergency relief supplies list, Liang Yu emphasized women's roles as professionals and protectors of the nation: "Not only medical workers in the pandemic, but also policewomen, firewomen, female snipers, female soldiers . . . female pilots and others working at their jobs need government-organized supplies of menstrual products . . . to better protect people and society."[5] This rhetoric might remind people that in the Maoist age (1949–1978), female workers in public factories and institutions had monthly subsidies called "hygiene allowance" (卫生费) to buy menstrual products. This was gradually abolished during the "reform and opening up" to establish a market economy which started in 1978. Maoist recognition of female biology that discarded period shame as backward or feudal is restructured to resist the sexualization/stigmatization of female bodies in the current post-reform age.

Although the authorities cannot openly reject socialist ideology, they are hostile to autonomous civil organizations, especially feminist ones. Women's representation in China is monopolized by the All-China Women's Federation, which was established in 1949 through annexing all existing women's organizations. Any other feminist autonomous civil organizations challenging this monopoly were portrayed as going against the regime. Stand By Her, as a nationally influential project organized with autonomous feminist ideals, is in itself a challenge to the authoritarian unitary system. This is especially so in light of the authorities' well-known negligence of duties in their own pandemic response.

The Women's Federation resorted to hijacking Liang's work. In February 2020, when Liang's team was working overtime organizing donations, the All-China Women's Federation pirated images from Liang's post for its own Weibo account alongside official projects.

They got the media involved to imply to the public that the project—made possible by autonomous public concerns for equality and justice—was government-sponsored and led by the Women's Federation. This theft of Liang and her team's work erases public contributions and public autonomy. Liang and her team didn't discover the piracy until March (2020), and she immediately posted her protests on Weibo, calling for public help. The theft aroused much anger among feminists and other supporters of Liang Yu. With thousands of reposts and wide criticism, the Federation finally deleted the post with the pirated figures (Liang 2020a). However, Liang's post accusing the Federation of piracy was censored before that, and anti-feminist forces on Weibo continued to state that the project was not initiated and run by Liang Yu but by the Federation. Moreover, the Federation might consider the hijacking of an acknowledgement or government endorsement of Liang Yu, as it has traditionally felt entitled to exert jurisdiction over all women's work in the entire country.

With the Stand By Her project, Liang Yu and other feminists called for adding menstrual products to the emergency relief supplies, allowing pads and tampons to be transported through the green channels. Right before Women's Day (March 8) 2020, the All-China Women's Federation announced that female hygiene products had been listed as emergency relief supplies. However, both Liang Yu and workers on the frontline later proved that these were still not allowed to enter through the green channels (Chenmi 2020). Despite constant appeals by feminists on Weibo, female hygiene was never included, while even tea was (Liang 2020b). The Federation sought to terminate the discussion with a lie, suggesting that instead of solving actual problems, the primary intention of the authorities is to silence criticism. The incident also indicated the Federation's marginal position in the Party-state system. It seems to have no power in either decision-making process or actual resources coordination.

In the second-wave of the pandemic in 2021, Liang and her team continued to provide tampons and pads to women on the frontline. In February 2021, Stand By Her released a free 200-page online handbook so that other grassroots organizers could benefit from their experience running the project (Standbyher 2021). The powerful support from women and the masses and the open transparency of information leave no opportunity for the authorities to hijack and usurp the fruit of these women's work, but only to recognize its existence, making this project one of real public benefit.

Courageous Women Confront the Information Blockade

On December 30, 2019, Ai Fen (艾芬), director of the Emergency Department of the Central Hospital of Wuhan, read a test report of a patient with pneumonia on which was written "SARS coronavirus." Shocked by the finding, Ai immediately reported it to the higher responsible departments and informed the medical staff of her department and the director of the Respiratory Department. She also sent the report with "SARS coronavirus" circled in red to her old classmate who, also a doctor, had asked Ai to confirm whether reports of infectious diseases related to the local Hunan Seafood Market, known as the initial birthplace of COVID-19, were true.

In the evening, the picture of the report with the red circle marked by Ai had spread. That was the source that Li Wenliang (李文亮) and seven other doctors used to alert the public, for which they were admonished by the police. They had to sign their names on the admonishment letter, acknowledging their fault and promising to stop transmitting any messages about the infectious disease.

As the initial leaker, Ai was chastised by leaders of the hospital: "As a professional, how can you ignore your principles and disciplines, spread rumors, and cause trouble?"[6] It was "as if the promising progress of the whole Wuhan city had been messed up by me alone," said Ai[7] (Gong 2020). Until January 16, 2020, the leader of the hospital insisted that the disease was "preventable, curable, and controllable," which was the official rhetoric across China until Zhong Nanshan (钟南山), the national respiratory authority, confirmed that it was infectious on January 20. Just four days later, the whole of Wuhan city was locked down.

Doctor Ai Fen's experience is just one example of the conflicts between medical professionalism and authoritarian vanity. Although women are openly required to meet higher standards in obtaining employment and promotion,[8] they still earn over half the jobs through diligent efforts. Their presence has maintained a comparatively modern professional space, in contrast with the conservative male-dominated political arena. In the COVID-19 response, in spite of a dictatorial information blockade and governmental malfeasance, there has been high professionalism and devotion among frontline workers, including medical staff and voluntary workers such as Liang Yu and many others. The information blockade continued after Wuhan was locked down, and the citizens had to resort to Weibo to share authentic scenes of their lives and to call for help. Meanwhile, the nationalist rhetoric threatened that the exposure of the negative side and individual difficulties would be considered treason. Resisting the information blockade, counter-voices rose online, with a remarkable number of feminists.

How destructive is information control to the public? The situation in the Wuhan Central Hospital is a representative example. After being scolded by her leader, Ai could do nothing but enhance precautions in her own department. She requested all doctors and nurses wear masks and protective suits (under their white coats, as these were not allowed) and distribute masks to all patients. As a result, the over-loaded Emergency Department and Respiratory

Department had fewer infectious cases, while in other departments, several medical experts died from coronavirus exposure, including the ophthalmologist Li Wenliang, who had also been admonished by the police for alerting the public about the coronavirus.[9]

In a later interview, Ai expressed regret for not being able to inform more people: "If I'd known of this [terrible result], I (*lao zi*) would have told everybody [regardless of the authorities]."[10] Ai used an arrogant and impudent first-person description to signify herself in Chinese, *lao zi* (老子), literally meaning "I, your father." The term is often used by men to imply a more empowered self. The wording exhibits an angry and rebellious emotion against authoritarian information control, and it has made her a national idol.

The interview was censored upon publication online, which triggered outrage among the public. People translated pieces of the article into English, German, Japanese, emojis, Morse code, Braille, and ancient Chinese writings such as zhuan shu calligraphy to circulate it, forming a marvelous spectacle online. This action was more of a protest than a spreading of information, as some versions had become unreadable.

The disasters in the COVID-19 response reflect an underlying systemic problem magnified by extreme circumstances. When frontline medical staff ran short of personal protective equipment and other supplies, public donations from all over China were accumulated and left in piles in the storage of Red Cross Society of China Wuhan Branch, which monopolized donations to the city. The bureaucratism and inefficiency of government institutions shocked the public. On January 29 (2020), major hospitals were forced to use their Weibo accounts to directly tell the public that they had run out of supplies. At the same time, a man was seen taking a box of masks into an official vehicle, saying it was for the leaders, and 30,000 masks were distributed to a private hospital without any COVID patients (Cui and Yang 2020). Due to heated public criticism, the government was finally forced to appoint a nongovernmental medicine and transportation corporation to take over the storage and circulation of donated materials.

Nurses, mostly female, are heavily exploited and discriminated against in the Chinese medical system, and they have faced even more perils throughout the coronavirus response. On January 26, Zhang Wanyan (张婉嬿), a female nurse from Wuhan Union Hospital, contacted a blogger on Weibo to expose the low-protection working conditions of nurses in her hospital. Without relevant training, they were told to collect samples from patients using throat swabs. Treatments were accomplished by nurses following doctors' instructions via intercoms, as doctors seldom showed up in the hospital's quarantine space. Women were thus exposed to risks at a much higher rate than men. This caused wide criticism from the public. Furthermore, on July 29 (2020), whistle-blower Zhang mysteriously fell to her death from her hospital building. The police denied the possibility of murder. To avoid provoking public outcry, the official announcement did not mention the name of the deceased nurse, and the keywords that had been searched heatedly on Weibo were censored. The person who posted Zhang's messages during the coronavirus response confirmed her death and posted many messages from other nurses about their harsh and exploitative conditions (Jiaowo 2020).

Under the information blockade, Weibo as a mass digital platform has played an important role. It was almost the only channel for ordinary citizens to ask for help. Feminist netizens also helped circulate any posts calling for help they could see on Weibo, forming a remarkable force for mutual aid.

Although the authorities in Wuhan announced that all coronavirus-infected patients were treated in hospitals, a large number of potential patients could not be tested and diagnosed as infected by COVID-19. Consequently, they could receive no medical treatment, confined to home in a locked-down city. On February 5, a 77-year-old grandfather learned how to use Weibo and sent his first message, "hello," to the world. Then he sent a second post calling for help. His daughter had already died of COVID-19, and he, his wife, and their thirteen-year-old granddaughter were infected but couldn't get diagnosed and treated. He pleaded for help to get his granddaughter hospitalized first (Laosu 2020). Due to great public concern, the family was hospitalized on February 7. On February 28, the grandfather died; both his wife and granddaughter survived.

On February 9, a video of a woman drumming a gong on the balcony of a high-rise apartment crying for help spread on Weibo. Again, due to public attention, she and her mother received medical treatment. However, those who posted what was happening around them not only needed to make tremendous efforts to prove authenticity but could also be insulted as "enemies of the nation." Nationalist rhetoric against foreign enemies politicized criticism and mutual aid among the public. It especially added to the predicament of women, at whom moral judgments and nationalist accusations were disproportionally aimed. A female writer in Wuhan, Fang (方方), released her diaries online during the lockdown period, which incurred attacks from government supporters. Although her diaries recorded her personal life and what she saw and heard online and were not overtly political, she was accused of humiliating the country with rumors and providing material for foreign enemies to attack China. As a result, Fang Fang's Weibo account was suspended. When her diaries were first published abroad in English as *Wuhan Diary: Dispatches from the Original Epicenter* (Fang Fang 2020), the cyberbullies against her attacked relentlessly. Even the woman who had drummed a gong and yelled from her balcony to get medical attention rebuked Fang Fang for mentioning her: "Don't write me into your work; I don't want to go abroad."[11]

Behind her attack on Fang Fang is a panic stemming from the witch hunt against "national enemies," especially women. The woman's repeated statements such as, "I am nobody but a minor citizen" and "I don't want to go abroad" betray a deep anxiety. She mistook the female writer as the cause of her panic, ignoring that speaking out and public mutual aid may have saved her life. Having received both praise and criticism for her attack on Fang Fang, she deleted all her posts and quit Weibo. In her last post, she observed: "It was too complicated. You all sound reasonable, so I don't know what to say … A virus could classify a person into a certain camp at any time, and then you would have enemies. It's horrible!"[12] She certainly sensed the dehumanizing political camps, but it was not the virus doing that; the virus only provided a fuse.

Misogynistic Propaganda and Feminist Counter-narratives

A news report during the pandemic showed male and female medical workers in a Wuhan hospital being served different meals. Men's meals had an extra dish as well as soup, fruit, and yoghurt, all lacking in meals served to the majority: female workers. The practice was praised by the reporter for its careful consideration of "avoiding waste."[13] Meanwhile, the military channel of China National Radio (2020) focused the spotlight on the only "Mr. Nurse" in the team, saying that "male nurses win an edge with better mental endurance and emotional control."[14]

These are just two among many examples of unequal treatment of female medical staff. A blatant discrimination against women was regarded as material for positive news coverage. Sexist rhetoric circulates freely with few sensing anything wrong with it until feminists challenge the public. Seeing government propaganda utilize the intensive labor of female workers to justify the current political system while misrepresenting them, feminists construct counternarratives in various formats.

Coverage of female workers often focuses on their bodies. Women's sacrifice as wives and mothers and misfortunes related to sexuality are highlighted. For example, there are nine-month-pregnant nurses required to work, a nurse returning to work ten days after a miscarriage, and female medical workers being shaved bald before being sent to the epicenter (Zijingshu 2020; *Wuhan Daily*, 2020; A. Chen 2020). Under the cover of praising women's sacrifice, there is reaffirmation of women's role in reproduction and sex, neglecting women's actual needs and the overexploitation of female bodies. As a feminist blogger states: "A female doctor who hasn't been pregnant or suffered miscarriages, when she intends to strive for primary worker's rights as a normal person, will find her space to speak tightened or even totally squeezed."[15] The superficial praise of women's sacrifice only normalizes their sacrifice. Feminist bloggers on Weibo expose, criticize, and protest against the injustice suffered by frontline female workers and the reductive, misogynistic misrepresentations.

Female manual laborers are even more likely to be erased. The construction of Huoshenshan Hospital (33,900 square meters) and Leishenshan Hospital (79,700 square meters) in ten days in the epicenter city of Wuhan are used as propaganda for China's authoritarian unitary system, which is at core patriarchal, women-excluding, and based on a hierarchy of men or, more euphuistically, "brothers." CCTV News (2020) paid respect to 40,000 "brothers" constructing these hospitals, turning blind eyes to the many female laborers working on the sites.

Unlike medical workers, the number of female manual laborers participating in the construction of the two hospitals has never been recorded. Male supremacists boasted of the masculinity behind the "China speed" that amazed the world. In response, a feminist marked all female laborers in a news picture taken on one of the hospital construction sites. Wearing work clothes and safety helmets, female laborers looked just like their male peers. The feminist could only identify the women by their long hair (possibly not counting short-haired women), and still identified at least half of the builders as women.[16] Another feminist blogger made a video about these female manual laborers, "Her Power in Huoshenshan" (Baolie 2020).

Identifying women by their longer hair reminds feminists of another misogynistic intention behind the forced head-shaving of frontline female nurses (and not their male counterparts): erasing women while utilizing their power. *Gansu Daily* posted on Weibo a video of female medical staff being shaved bald before setting off to Wuhan, using the scenes of the weeping nurses as propaganda. Although it is said to be done for reasons of hygiene, the only male nurse in the team was not only allowed to keep his crewcut, but also is the only one in the group photo who wears a high-grade N95 respirator mask. This aroused so much criticism that *Gansu Daily* deleted the video.

The authorities did occasionally acknowledge women's contributions. However, the symbol of their female identity, long hair, was removed. The language praising them either stressed their uteruses and reproductive roles to downplay their professionalism or integrated them into the narratives of "brothers." In other words, their identities as professional women were not recognized. This prevents their contributions from earning increased opportunities for future women and even for themselves. While even pregnant women were still working on the frontline, the local government in Jinan (Shandong province) had already launched an initiative urging mothers to apply for leave from their jobs to care for children because of delayed school semesters (*Jinan Lives* 2020).

Autonomous feminist criticism of misogynistic propaganda increased and intensified so much that a feminist cultural uprising was on its way. Taking over a token girl puppet from the propaganda institution, they resurrected it collectively and redefined it as their own.

"Jiang Shanjiao, Do you Get Your Period?"

On February 17, the Communist Youth League (a Party organization for any government agenda concerning teenagers) promoted a pair of virtual cartoon idols as mascots on its official Weibo account. Jiang Shanjiao (Lovely Land), and her younger brother Hong Qiman (Abundant Red Flags), both have names that allude to a poem of Mao Zedong. The League was trying to make the nationalist and patriotic spirit attractive to contemporary teens by using popular cultural forms. They expected teens to conform eagerly to the established system just as fans pursue their idols. With rising criticism of the information blockade, inefficiency of government management, and misogynistic propaganda, the authorities sought to enhance national solidarity.

The images of the idols, crudely made, are unlikely to appeal to the target audience. The authorities seem to ignore the fierce competition in the modern cartoon industry, which has developed high aesthetic standards. The idols made by the Communist Youth League use blunt racial and gender stereotypes with a combination of cheap Japanese cartoon elements that stereotypically symbolize Chinese nationality and femininity. The hands of the girl, Jiang Saojiao, are terrifyingly blood-red and bony. When the authorities so wrongly assume they can earn public praise with such low-grade cultural products, the failure of their propaganda campaign is inevitable.[17]

On February 18, 2020, feminist blogger Why It Goes on Forever (为什么它永无止境) posted just one sentence: "Jiang Shanjiao, do you get your period?" alluding to online arguments about period shame evoked by the Stand By Her project. Under the original post, many women began to address questions to Jiang Shanjiao. Before the post was censored the next day, it received more than 10,000 replies and 100,000 reposts, making it a massive outlet for Chinese women to share experiences of sex discrimination.

There were the questions they faced throughout their education: "Jiang Shanjiao, can you keep up with boys in high school?" "Jiang Shanjiao, did you get a PhD to find a better husband?" "Jiang Shanjiao, do you also need to score 200 points higher than male students to be admitted to public security academies?"

There were questions degrading their bodies as commodities: "Jiang Shanjiao, are you devalued goods after twenty-five?" "Jiang Shanjiao, are you second-hand goods after divorce?" "Jiang Shanjiao, after abortion, are you just like a house where a tenant has died?" "Jiang Shanjiao, are you a virgin?" There were questions of victim-blaming familiar to women around the globe: "Jiang Shanjiao, wearing such a short skirt, who could you blame for photographing you secretly?" "Jiang Shanjiao, are you dressed up like this to tempt Hong Qiman?"

There were work-related questions: "Jiang Shanjiao, did you sleep with your boss to gain a promotion?" "Jiang Shanjiao, how could you balance life and work after getting married?" "Jiang Shanjiao, will you respond or pretend not to listen when your male colleagues tell dirty jokes?" "Jiang Shanjiao, we are just joking. Why are you so sensitive?"

There were questions with Chinese characteristics: "Jiang Shanjiao, if you had a brother, would you have been born?"[18] "Jiang Shanjiao, what did your brother do with the money donated to support your schooling?"[19] "Jiang Shanjiao, can women sit at the table to eat in your hometown?"[20] "Jiang Shanjiao, will your words be censored by the law?" "Jiang Shanjiao, will our questions for you survive the night?"[21] At last, there is an attempt to incorporate Jiang Shanjiao as one of their own: "Jiang Shanjiao, will you cry just like me reading all these?"

By absorbing all the suffering of women, fictional Jiang Shanjiao was infused with real meaning. As a token girl forged by the authorities with no personality, she couldn't represent Chinese women; after she became a real woman, she was deleted by the authorities as if she had never existed, just as they have done with many feminist posts.

However, by collective recreation, women have kept Jiang Shanjiao to themselves. As a representation of a real female being, she could never be erased or taken from women. The blogger who triggered the Jiang Shanjiao incident reflected on the process:

> You can't delete collective emotion by deleting its carriers ... Discourse creates discourse automatically, and it has nothing to do with my original question ... If not me, there would be someone else asking. If you do not ask questions, there will be no answers.[22]

The name "Jiang Shanjiao" became commonly used in feminist posts and products. For example, Saidongzhe (2020) made a video, "Jiang Shanjiao, Do They Tell You the Same?" to expose period shame, body shame, and misogynistic public discourse. It has been viewed more than 15 million times.

Another significance of "questioning Jiang Shanjiao" lies in the fact that it also terminated the long-time steering of fandom culture by the authorities. Fandom culture, enjoyed mostly by teens, especially girls, had become a tool of oppression through government control. "Questioning Jiang Shanjiao" warned the authorities of the risks involved in the entertainmentization of politics.

Previously, many overseas scholars, including those from Hong Kong and Taiwan, believed that popular or fandom culture booming among Chinese youth signified resistance to government propaganda (Lu 2018: 10). This assumption collapsed during the Hong Kong protest in 2019 when the "fan girls' crusade" supported "Brother China."[23] ("Brother China" replacing "Mother China" corresponds with the country's increasing virilization and reinforcement of male dominance in nationalist narratives.)

During the 2019 Hong Kong pro-democracy protests, China's state-owned media, including the *People's Daily*, promoted "Brother China" as a personification of the nation and solicited "fan girls" to protect "Brother China" as intensely (and irrationally) as they pursue pop idols. The authorities represented by the China Communist Youth League encouraged "fan girls" and other youth to launch an online war against protestors in Hong Kong. Ironically, the "fan girls' crusade" relied on VPNs (technically illegal in China) to get them across to their battlefields: international networks such as Twitter and Facebook. With fanaticism as their fandom culture was for the first time recognized by the highest authority in China, the fan girls launched fierce verbal attacks at those who were probably Hong Kong's version of themselves.

The authorities' utilization of fan girls was possible because of female marginalization. Teenage girls were excited about the illusory empowerment of being supported by the authorities. More often, cyberattacks and harassment are launched by men in a women-hating culture in the name of nationalism and patriotism. On June 9, 2010, netizens launched a spam attack on the fan websites of Korean pop group Super Junior because some fans caused a disturbance at the Shanghai Expo, which was called "Holy War" by the participants. In a promotional video for the "Holy War" on YouTube,[24] participants were called "patriots from various national online forums," which were all typical men's cyber spaces. Teenage girls pursuing their idols have always been humiliated as "brainless," or "fandom bitches" (饭圈母狗). The internet, though under minute surveillance, has never censored insults or even terrorist proclamations against women. In 2016, with the agreement to employ Terminal High Altitude Area Defense (THAAD) in South Korea reached by U.S. and Korean governments, the "patriots" achieved final success. Many girls and women announced on Weibo that they loved their country more than their (Korean pop) idols and would quit pursuing the idols because of Korea's anti-China behavior.

However, in 2019, Houston Rockets general manager Daryl Morey tweeted in support of the Hong Kong protests and the spokesman of China Ministry of Foreign Affairs urged NBA fans to boycott the coming matches in China. The stadiums were still crowded with Chinese male fans both in Shanghai and Shenzhen.[25] Ironically, among these male fans, many had accused fan girls of treason. Although stadiums crowded with male fans were not expected by the authorities, they did nothing against these men. Such double standards from the authorities are widely exposed by Weibo feminists, causing many women to wake up from nationalist illusions.

The "questioning of Jiang Shanjiao" marked the end of authorities' massive steering of female emotions and energies using pop culture. The authorities may forget (or never understand) the nature of fandom. It is the recreational power among fans, who produce "semiotic productivity into some form of textual production that can circulate among—and thus help to define—the fan community" (Fiske 1992, 30). In other words, as long as you have released the idols, they will be redescribed and recreated through the collective imagination, just as with Jiang Shanjiao. The national tokens may work well temporarily with high-handed power but cannot not replace autonomous and collective fandom creations in the long run. "Brother China" and other official virtual idols would be forgotten unless public recreations changed the core permanently, taking them over from the hands of the authorities and making them the people's. Public recreations, however, are unpredictable. Women took over Jiang Shanjiao while "Brother China" and "Hong Qiman" soon died because of their monolithic rigidity. After "Questioning Jiang Shanjiao," the inspection team of the Party required the Communist Youth League to stop entertainizing politics immediately.[26]

Feminist presence on Weibo has successfully challenged the authorities and, perhaps even more importantly, gained the support of millions of ordinary women. Weibo feminists are capable competitors with the authorities' nationalist and patriarchal agenda when it comes to influencing public opinion. Women's presence at the forefront of the coronavirus response, and transparent and effective feminist actions and insights, fueled a movement supported by the massive numbers of people reachable online, and this work continues to expand.

Works Cited

Baolie [@暴烈甜心小鳄鱼毛毛]. (2020, February 3). 火神山她力量 [Her Power on Huo Shenshan]. Weibo. https://weibo.com/5288987897/IssFu3ArI?type=comment

CCTV News [@央视新闻]. (2020, April). 致敬4万多位”火雷兄弟” [Pay Respect to 40,000 Brothers on Leishenshan and Huoshenshan]. Weibo. https://weibo.com/tv/show/1034:4490732854247430?from=old_pc_videoshow.

Chen, Aria. (2020, February 21). Video of Female Medics in China Having Their Heads Shaved Sparks Backlash Over Propaganda in the Coronavirus Fight. *TIME*. https://time.com/5788592/weibo-women-coronavirus/.

Chen, Chen. (2020, July 13). "Stand By Her:" Chinese Feminist Rhetoric during the COVID-19 Pandemic. DRC: Digital Rhetoric Collaborative. www.digitalrhetoriccollaborative.org/2020/07/13/stand-by-her-chinese-feminist-rhetoric-during-the-covid-19-pandemic/.

Chenmi [@沉迷种树的果喵]. (2020, May 20). “姐妹战疫安心行动”纪实 [A Review of Stand By Her Project]. Weibo. https://card.weibo.com/article/m/show/id/2309404506748722479644?_wb_client_=1.

China Daily. (2020, February 2). 武汉志愿者车队在行动，护送医务人员上下班 [Volunteers in Wuhan Are Taking Actions, Driving Medical Workers to and from Work]. ChinaDaily.com. http://cn.chinadaily.com.cn/a/202002/02/WS5e36aa6da3107bb6b579cabe.html.

Cui, Huiying and Yang, Kaiqi. (2020, April 15). 复盘舆论漩涡中的武汉红十字会 [Wuhan Red Cross Society in the Whirlpool of Public Criticism: A Review]. infzm. www.infzm.com/contents/181565

Czymara, C. S., Langenkamp, A., and T. Cano. (2020). "Cause for concerns: gender inequality in experiencing the COVID-19 lockdown in Germany." *European Societies*, DOI: 10.1080/14616696.2020.1808692

Debbie-Qijiang [@Debbie-齐姜]. (2020, February 13). 疫情期间被某些媒体挪用的女性身体 [Female Bodies Hijacked by Some Media in the Pandemic Period]. Weibo. https://m.weibo.cn/status/4471519852359270?

Fiske, John. (1992). The Cultural Economy of Fandom. In Lisa A. Lewis (Ed.), *The Adoring Audience: Fan Culture and Popular Media* (pp. 30–49). Routledge.

Fortier, N. (2020). "COVID-19, gender inequality, and the responsibility of the state." *International Journal of Wellbeing*, 10(3), 77–93.

Gong, Jingqi. (2020, March 10). 发哨子的人：如果这些医生都能够得到及时的提醒，或许就不会有这一天 [The One Who Distributed the Whistles: If the Doctors Could Have Been Warned in Time, Today Could Be Different]. 中国医院人文建设 [China Hospital Humanitarian Construction]. www.yyrw.org.cn/e/action/ShowInfo. php?classid=5&id=2256.

Hong Fincher, Leta. (2018). *Betraying Big Brother: The Feminist Awakening in China*. Verso.

Jiaowo [@叫我安然君]. (2020, July 29). 协和医院一护士坠楼 [A Nurse Fell to Death in Wuhan Union Hospital]. Weibo. https://weibo. com/5581654880/JdseccrJT?type=comment#_rnd1597069601190.

Jinan Lives [@济南生活]. (2020, February 17). 济南向各单位倡议：延迟开学期间支持双职工家庭以女方为主在家看孩子 [Jinan Municipal Government Advised Wives in Dual-Worker Families to Apply for Staying at Home for Childcare during Delayed School Semesters]. Weibo. https://weibo.com/5329116942/IuCch7MHa?type=comment#_rnd1597072418211.

Ke, Li. (2020, March 8). *2.8万女性驰援湖北，占总数2/3* [28,000 Women Ride to Hubei Providing Emergency Support, Making up 2/3 of the Total]. Chang Jiang Daily-Chang Jiang Net. www.cjrbapp.cjn.cn/p/166459.html.

Laosu [@老苏8811]. (2020, February 5). 武汉肺炎患者求助 [Calling for Help from a Wuhan Patient]. Weibo. https://weibo.com/6350728521 /IsIhe0PZm?type=comment#_rnd1597069778557.

Liang, Yu [@梁钰 stacey]. (2020a, March 16). 之前"姐妹战疫安心行动"项目进展明细公示图片反复未经允许滥用的事 [About the Previous Abuse of the Publicized Items Details of Stand By Her Project without Permission]. Weibo. https://m.weibo.cn/status/4483031601294747?

Liang, Yu. [@梁钰 stacey]. (2020b, June 24). 茶叶及其包装材料纳入了河南省疫情期间的生活物资清单，还有红头文件 [Tea Leaves and their Package Materials Were Included in the Emergency List in Pandemic Periods in Henan Province, with the Official Document]. Weibo. https://weibo.com/1306934677/J86HU1v9d?type=comment#_rnd1597067344710.

Lu, Chen. (2018). *Chinese Fans of Japanese and Korean Pop Culture: Nationalistic Narratives and International Fandom.* Routledge.

Military Channel of China National Radio [@央广军事]. (2020, April 9). 火神山医院的护士先生 [Mr. Nurse in the Huoshenshan Hospital]. Weibo. https://weibo.com/1728148193/ICxTxCnyB?type=comment.

Morse, M. M. and G. Anderson. (2020, April 4). "The Shadow Pandemic: How The COVID-19 Crisis Is Exacerbating Gender Inequality". UN Foundation: https://unfoundation.org/blog/post/shadow-pandemic-how-covid19-crisis-exacerbating-gender-inequality/.

Qiaoluo [@敲锣的我]. (2020, May 15). 太复杂了 [It Was Too Complicated]. Weibo. https://weibo.com/u/3953644365?is_hot=1#_rnd1596510566322.

Saidongzhe [@赛冬者]. (2020, May). 江山娇，他们也会对你说吗？ [Jiang Shanjiao, Do They Tell You the Same?]. Weibo. https://weibo.com/tv/show/1034:4502481867046929?from=old_pc_videoshow

Standbyher [@予她同行_Standbyher]. (2021, February). 姐妹战疫安心行动项目操作手册 [Standard Operating Procedure of "Sisters Combating Pandemic" Project]. Weibo. https://weibo.com/5627318598/K0pDV6YXo?sudaref=www.baidu.com&display=0&retcode=6102&type=comment#_rnd1625502442714.

UN Women. (2020). *The First 100 Days of the COVID-19 Outbreak in Asia and the Pacific: A Gender Lens.* www2.unwomen.org/-/media/field%20office%20eseasia/docs/publications/2020/04/ap_first_100-days_covid-19-r02.pdf?la=en&vs=3400.

Why It Goes On Forever [@为什么它永无止境]. (2020, February 18). 这事真的火得莫名其妙，删得也莫名其妙 [It Arose Suddenly and Was Deleted Suddenly]. Weibo. https://weibo.com/3102117384/IuKrTgCp3?type=comment.

World Economic Forum. (2021, March 30). *Global Gender Gap Report, 2021.* www.weforum.org/reports/global-gender-gap-report-2021

Wuhan Daily. (2020, February 12). 流产10天后，武汉90后女护士重回一线 [Ten Days after Miscarriage, the Young Nurse Returned to Her Position on the Frontline]. Guancha. www.guancha.cn/politics/2020_02_12_535828.shtml

Xie, Lei. (2020, February 17). 疫情下的武汉咖啡馆：就算店垮了，最后一杯咖啡也给医生 [Wuhan Cafe in Pandemic: Even if the Cafe Goes Bankrupt, the Last Cup Would Be Offered to the Doctors]. The Beijing News. www.bjnews.com.cn/inside/2020/02/17/690861.html.

Zijingshu [@紫荆树]. (2020, February 15). 怀孕9个月护士不顾家人反对，奔赴在抗疫一线 [Nurse with Nine-Month Pregnancy Working on the Frontline of Coronavirus Response, Regardless of the Opposition from Families]. Weibo. https://weibo.com/1198220993/IuhnDzOt0?type=comment#_rnd1597071724587.

2

Spreading Feminism Online

On February 10, 2021, the eve of China's most important (Spring Festival/Chinese New Year) holiday, all online accounts of Lin Maomao (林毛毛), from blogs to video platforms, suddenly disappeared. Such swift action involving many companies suggests executive orders from high government authorities. An influential feminist with almost one million followers, Lin Maomao had been posting for nearly ten years. In September 2020, she was forbidden from posting on her Weibo account for one year; she soon registered a new one under the same name and continued spreading her feminist thoughts widely online, until this most recent and more extreme action against her words.

Born in a village near Tianjin, China, and living in Germany for decades, Lin is now cyberly exiled from her native country. Chinese authorities are strongly against autonomous feminism. They even put young women in jail for planning to distribute anti-sexual harassment stickers on subways (Hong Fincher 2018). Lin's case, however, is different. She never called for action or directly criticized the government. Posts are about her personal life: love, sex, marriage, family, and her daughters. She believes in women's ability to solve their own problems through self-awareness without any need for politics. So why were the authorities intent on wiping her words out of China? No authorities, even authoritarian ones, can fully censor everything in today's digital age, but they did take extreme measures to stop Lin from addressing Chinese women directly. What was it that she said?

This chapter analyzes content from a huge body of feminist posts on Weibo and divides them into two kinds: First, the feminist subversion of history includes the unlearning of the official narrative, the rediscovery of women's past, and the significance of history in Chinese culture. Second, the current agenda of Weibo feminism turns feminist politics to actions in women's everyday lives, including refusing marriage and Confucian filial obligations, insisting on inheritance rights, and gaining autonomy in reproduction. Why personal-level agendas such as Lin's are so threatening to the authorities will be explored.

Although Chinese feminism has a long history and diverse present, Weibo feminism takes an unprecedented route. It is different from working under the umbrella of All-China Women's Federation or with NGOs supported by foreign funds such as the Ford Foundation, from the performance of *The Vagina Monologues* in colleges, and from young activists occupying men's toilets to call attention to unequal resources. Overall, they aim to reform existing political, social, or cultural mechanisms.

Weibo feminism, however, has given up on reformation. Its goal in pointing out the inequality and injustice women face serves only to awaken women. The awakened use their bodies and personal lives as fortresses, breaking away from the existing mechanisms. They do not directly confront the superstructures (the Party-state or authoritarianism), but their personal choices widen the crevices of patriarchal constructs, shaking their foundations.

For nearly a decade, government censors had paid no attention to Lin Maomao. Authorities did not previously consider that the personal revolt of individuals posed any threat. However, it has now become obvious that wide female disobedience, or scattered revolutions, are taking shape. Blocking Lin Maomao cannot stop this, as thousands of other accounts are now inspiring women in similar ways.

The Chinese Cult of History

Approximately 2,500 years ago, a man Fan Xuanzi (范宣子) asked a wise man, "What is immortality?" After refuting the probable response of family descendants, the wise man said, "The highest is the establishment of morality (for people to follow); then comes the establishment of merits (that benefit the nation); then, it is the establishment of words . . . these are immortality."[1]

These "three immortalities" (三不朽) (as the eternal bliss of heaven in Christianity) are the ultimate meaning of life in the traditional Confucian society of China. Confucius said something similar: "A gentleman is troubled by the thought of his name not being mentioned after his death."[2] The ancient romantic poet Qu Yuan (340 B.C.–278 B.C.) also lamented in his famous *Li Sao*: "Growing old as I am, I'm afraid of not being able to establish my name."[3] Si Maqian (145 B.C.–unknown), a historian, explained in a letter why he, when in trouble, chose castration rather than death to remain alive for the accomplishment of his historical book, *Shi Ji*, "establishing one's name is the ultimate of one's deeds."[4] When Wen Tianxiang, a minister during the Song dynasty, decided to be killed rather than submit to the Mongolian Yuan dynasty in 1283, he considered the glory of his name higher than his life: "From ancient times to today, who has avoided death? I'd rather that my loyalty would leave a page in the annals."[5] In a passage of *tanci*, a musical storytelling art, by Yang Shen (1448–1559), struggling for historical immortality is questioned: "(For) several lines on the annals, numerous tombs lie in the wilderness."[6] All these suggest the traditional Chinese attitude that historical records surpass life itself as the ultimate meaning.

If the immortality of one's name in traditional Chinese culture equals the immortality of one's soul in religious cultures, then the institutions in charge of compiling histories function as a church. The compilation and interpretation of history has always been dominated by the authorities. They determine what kind of morality, merits, and words can be immortalized positively in history books. Women are deprived of eligibility to strive for historical immortality because, according to Confucian moral doctrines, "Women's words are not supposed to circulate outside the family door."[7]

Compiled histories of righteousness serve as models for current lives and sources of legitimacy for current politics. The significance of history in Chinese culture explains why subverting and reconstructing history is essential for Chinese feminists. It is, however, a new step, as deep, reflexive emancipation of the mind, unlearning and subverting patriarchal histories, becomes a starting point to develop the current Weibo feminist agenda.

Restoring Women's Words

Who does the grand history and elegant literature belong to? Who are the people experiencing glorious and turbulent ages? Who is acting hero, and who does the hero intend to save? . . . They can be anybody, but [under any circumstance] cannot refer to women only. . . . Heroes cannot be women only, and even those who are suffering cannot be women only. . . . Women's sufferings are forever trivial and incidental.[8]

Wuming 2021

Women only appear in minor and otherized roles in patriarchal histories. The lack of women's independent narratives in history disturbs many Weibo feminists. Delving into ancient texts and archaeological evidence, feminists are restoring women's "three immortalities": their morality, merits, and words, which were once deleted and distorted.

Her name was lost for more than three thousand years, until her tomb was found in 1976. She was a military leader who defeated foreign invaders, a high priestess offering sacrifices to divine ancestors and transferring messages between heaven and Earth, a ruler of her own manor, and the spouse of a king, though they usually lived separately on their respective lands. Her tomb was filled with bronze vessels, weapons, and jade and shell ornaments from thousands of miles away. Her name is Fu Hao (妇好).

She is nothing like the empresses, queens, or concubines in the royal courts of later times, though mainstream historical interpretations, Western and Chinese, tend to implant her in that system. Fu Hao was buried alone rather than with her male spouse and with ritual vessels and weapons signifying only her own power. Patriarchal marriage is often taken as a civilized and advanced mechanism compared with the primitivism of the past (Chen 2016). Under this premise, to understand the authentic power and sexual relations of an aristocratic woman three thousand years ago is challenging.

Women in pre-Confucian China enjoyed freedom and power. Weibo feminists have dug up ancient matrilineal histories and philosophies while voicing stringent criticism of Confucianism. Fu Hao lived around 1300 B.C. during the Shang dynasty, when women exerted high religious and political power. Around 1100 B.C., the Shang dynasty was overthrown by the marginal kingdom of Zhou, which observed patriarchal norms later compiled as the Rites of Zhou (周礼), from which Confucianism originated. Zhou's replacement of Shang marked the beginning of huge decline in Chinese women's social status. Aristocratic women were deprived of the usage of bronze ritual vessels for their funerals (Zuo and Yang 2017), which suggests that political power became a solely male privilege. The rulers of Zhou were fiercely against and vilified Shang's custom of women possessing political influence (W. Li 2017).

Confucius (551 B.C.–479 B.C) combined historical and fictional rituals, moralities, politics, and literature into the Confucian classics, which were dignified by later dynasties as orthodoxy. These have dominated Chinese lives ever since. Intellectuals throughout Chinese history, from Kong Anguo (孔安国) (156 B.C.–74 B.C.), a remote heir of Confucius, to Wang Fuzhi (王夫之), a seventeenth-century philosopher, have mentioned that Confucius destroyed the majority of the books he used to compile his own writings. Chinese researchers have denied this, however, arguing that this was some kind of metaphor (S. Wang 2020; Zhao 2018). Whether Confucius is responsible or not, the fact remains that pre-Confucianism matriarchal classics have been lost.

The illustrious high status of Fu Hao and women before her, along with records and philosophical underpinnings of matrilineal civilization, have been lost. Although there is archeological evidence, what it suggests is beyond mainstream imagination. With the findings of Bronze Age archeological site Sanxingdui in Sichuan, people were so amazed by the advanced artistry in bronze, ivory, and clay that there was a hashtag on Weibo discussing whether Sanxingdui was an alien civilization. A feminist blogger ironized, "Sanxingdui is not alien, but (even more inconceivable to most): matriarchal"[9] (Chuan 2021). Among other evidence, most tombs in Sanxingdui only contain one body rather than a couple, suggesting marriage didn't exist or was not important (Xiao and Wu 2010).

In addition to archaeological findings, a final relic of Chinese matriarchal philosophy can be found in the *Dao De Jing* (道德经):

> When the Great Dao (natural way) ceased to be observed, benevolence and righteousness came into vogue; then appeared wisdom and shrewdness, and there ensued great hypocrisy. When the harmony of kinships was broken, the manifestation of filial sons and caring parents began; when the states fell into disorder, loyal ministers appeared.[11]

These lines are perhaps the most overtly anti-Confucian in Taoism. "Benevolence" or *ren* (仁) (of the ruler, or of the superior to the

Figure 2.1 A feminist artist on Weibo, Yichuanyuebai [@一川月白Lina], illustrates the patriarchal destruction and occupation of matrilineal cultural treasures. "Crown" © 一川月白 Lina. All rights reserved.[10]

inferior), "righteousness" or *yi* (义) (of one men to another equal men), "being filial" or *xiao* (孝) (sons to their parents), and "loyalty" or *zhong* (忠) (of the inferior to the superior) are core moral codes of Confucianism, whose most distinct feature is eliminating universal morality in favor of each rank in the hierarchical system living according to its own virtues and moral requirements. This hierarchal moral system mainly serves to regulate benefits and status among men. Women are subsidiary to fathers and husbands, conforming to men's wishes. The only specific moral obligation for women is abstinence or faithfulness. The *Dao De Jing* repudiates Confucian moral requirements as hypocritical pretexts and deviations from natural justice and harmony. Discussion of this issue is widespread among Weibo feminists.[12]

Because Marxist historical ideology is influential in China, especially Engels' *The Origin of the Family, Private Property and the State* (1884), the existence of matriarchal societies preceding patriarchy is common knowledge for most Chinese people. However, the mainstream historical outlook discards matriarchal societies as primitive and uncivilized. Typically, historical research in China predetermines patriarchal monogamy as advanced and civilized in contrast to primitivism, and even equates patriarchy with civilization without any questioning or even evidence of greater progress (Chen 2016). Weibo feminists oppose such opinions, unearthing and piecing together archeological clues. For example, one feminist blogger notes that Fu Hao's era (the Shang dynasty) had higher social productivity than the subsequent Zhou dynasty with its patriarchal norms: "The capital of Shang covered 30 square kilometers and that of Zhou less than 3 square kilometers."[13]

Western research works such as *The Chalice and the Blade* by Riane Eisler, *Das Mutterrecht* by Johann Jakob Bachofen, and the writings of archeologist Marija Gimbutas are also referred to. One feminist blogger made videos to introduce *The Chalice and the Blade*, in which she gave a vivid introduction and interpretation of the trial of Orestes (Shuangla 2021). These bloggers and their readers formed a topic community or (superchat/超话) for research on matrilineal societies.[14] Though feminist superchat is inclined to be blocked, intersectional ones as matrilineal history and loving-women literature are preserved.

Confucian patriarchy initiated the annihilation of women on various levels. First, the actual killing of female babies began, the first textual record of which dates to the Warring States Period (403 B.C.– 221 B.C.): "People celebrate the birth of sons and kill newborns if they are daughters."[15] Detailed regional methods for female infanticide and accounts of women being sold, bought, rented, raped, forced to commit suicide, and many other persecutions in ancient China are also cited by Weibo feminists (Hongli 2019; Shangshen 2020).

Another kind of annihilation of women involves erasing them from history. One example involves two women who rebelled against Confucian doctrines and were erased until recent historical rediscovery. Wang Zhenyi (王贞仪) was born to an intellectual bureaucrat's family in 1768. Thanks to her family, she was blessed with numerous books in mathematics, astronomy, medicine, literature, and Western science. As her father and grandfather held posts in different places, she followed her family all over the country and even learned horse-riding and archery from a Mongolian officer's wife. Ching Shih, seven years younger than Wang, was not so lucky. She belonged to the deeply discriminated caste Dan Jia (疍家) that lived on ships floating on the South China Sea, not allowed to settle on the bank. She first became a prostitute and later a renowned pirate.

As an astronomer, mathematician, scientist, and doctor, Wang explained phenomena such as solar and lunar eclipses, writing many research articles. However, she struggled to balance her scientific enthusiasm and Confucian norms for women. She burned a considerable portion of her own works before death, fearing that content not conforming to Confucian doctrines would bring her insults. She died at 29, and most of her works were lost.

Ching Shih married a pirate leader Zheng Yi and is therefore also known as Zheng Yi Sao (郑一嫂) (wife of Zheng Yi). She took over her husband's Red Flag Fleet after he died. Soon, with her strict pirate laws and wise management, her pirate fleet became one of the most successful in history, ruling more than a thousand ships and 80,000 sailors. She set the law that pirates who raped female captives would be put to death. Her fleet defeated the Qing dynasty navy, as well as Western fleets, many times. She eventually accepted the amnesty of the Qing dynasty and spent the rest of her life as a lawful citizen.

But as soon as Zheng Yi Sao landed from the sea, she was degraded by Confucian social norms. As a pirate, she was recorded as the leader of the Pirate Confederation, made up of six fleets, and was at least a co-commander of the Red Flag Fleet with her second husband, Zhang Bao (who was also her first husband Zheng Yi's adopted son). However, after accepting the amnesty of the Qing dynasty, by the Confucian doctrine, Zhang Bao was endowed with an official post while she received only an honorary Madame title as the officer's wife. In 1840, when Zhang Bao had died and Zheng was in her sixties, Lin Zexu[16] advised the Emperor to abolish Zheng's honorary Madame title. Apart from her notorious past as a pirate leader, one important reason is that by marrying again after her first husband died, she violated the Confucian abstinence doctrine set for women. The emperor approved the proposal and Zheng's title was eventually revoked (K. Wang 2019, 86). In the later dramatization of this pirate history in Hong Kong's popular culture, such as the film *The Pirate* (1973) or TV drama *Captain of Destiny* (2015), Zheng Yi Sao was marginalized and Zhang Bao became the center of the narratives.

Zheng Yi Sao's name went into oblivion in China, but was circulated legendarily in the West. There were a few official Chinese records about the amnesty of pirates mentioning her, and one of them, Jing Hai Fen Ji (1830) by Yuan Yonglun (袁永纶), was translated by a German scholar Charles Fred Neumann into English and published as *History of the Pirates Who Infested the China Sea from 1807 to 1810* (1831). From these records, Zheng Yi Sao's name has spread to a number of pirate histories in the West, though sometimes they are not free of orientalist exaggerations (K. Wang 2019, 88). Zheng Yi Sao's image went into literature, with Jorge Luis Borges' short story "The Widow Ching, Lady Pirate" (1935), and film, with *Pirates of the Caribbean: At World's End* (2007), which directly led to a modern rediscovery of this historical female pirate leader in China.

The miserable lives of women and their disappearance in histories are predetermined under Confucian patriarchal culture across regions, social classes, and educational backgrounds. Illustrious patriarchal families could not guarantee their daughters a room for writing, and dominating a sea and intimidating Westerners also does not earn women even one page in nationalist history. What women's histories convey to women today is that female identity is the basis to understanding and reconstructing their lives.[17]

Weibo feminists associate their criticism of Confucian patriarchy and reflections on matrilineal culture with the current social reality, bringing subversive criticism to the root of Chinese patriarchal politics at the family level. Today, the majority of Chinese families are still dominated by Confucian norms. However, the youth of today are not content with the myth of "caring parents" and "filial offspring." The young generation can receive advice from Weibo feminists that they could never imagine before: the anti-filial-obligation agenda of feminism.

Reconstructing the History of Chinese Feminism

Every dynasty in China was enthusiastic about compiling histories to support the politics of its time. The Party-state is no different. The official version of China's modern and contemporary history is placed alongside Marxism, Maoism, and the theories of Deng Xiaoping as a part of the field called "Politics," which is compulsory for all college students. It is part of exams for entry into graduate school, the teaching profession, and any public office.

What history conveys about women or feminism is the "up-down" (自上而下) liberation myth that Chinese women have already been liberated by the Party-state, who sent national will in the form of laws and policies from the high, saving Chinese women from miserable premodern oppression. The myth aims to persuade the public that because of the Party-state's historical merits in promoting social progress (including liberating women), it deserves the support of the masses. It teaches that women's emancipation has been achieved at least at the state level, so that fundamental systemic changes are no longer necessary. It is also said that Western women liberated themselves, but Chinese women *were liberated*. In this way, the passive role Chinese women were said to have played during the process of liberation was responsible for any existing inequality—all the blames are attributed to Chinese women not being responsible or self-reliant enough. Any problems still bothering Chinese women must stem from their own personal flaws—

it seems to be a universal rhetoric across the globe oppressing feminist yelling, from neoliberal capitalist societies to the Party-state of China.

This emphasis on the "different path" of Chinese feminism vis-à-vis Western feminism, with Chinese feminism initiated and accomplished by the Party as part of national and class liberation (Wesoky 2016, 55) serves to alienate Chinese women from international feminist movements and ideas. Overall, that Western experience cannot be applied to the Chinese situation is a reasonable claim. But this intentional estrangement from global feminism serves a political aim of nationalistic loyalty. Sino-Western political and ideological binarism leads to the neglect of feminism in other countries, missing opportunities to collaborate. There is also long-standing negation of any universal value to Chinese women's achievements.

The Women's Federation advocates "self-respect" (自尊) and "self-reliance" (自强) of women: "We want to have each individual assume her own responsibilities and be socially responsible," said a leader (Wesoky 2016, 60), although it is not specified in which ways Chinese women, whose labor force participation had been over 70 percent in the 1990s, have not been responsible enough.[18] The Federation blames women for the existing inequality rather than confronting structural and cultural exploitation.

Huang Lin, editor of the journal *Feminism in China* (中国女性主义), sought to create a "smiley Chinese feminism" which apparently accords with the government's promotion of a "harmonious society" (和谐社会). In Chinese academia, "feminism" is ususally translated as *nüxing zhuyi* (女性主义), meaning *-ism* of female gender, avoiding the more political *nüquan* (女权), meaning women's rights. Chinese women are required to strive in social production, be independent and self-reliant, and keep smiling—that is, be approachable, usable, exploitable, and manipulable. With such ideas, it is no wonder that even with high female participation in social production as professionals and technical workers, gender inequality in China worsens year by year.

To establish an autonomous feminist agenda to actually benefit women, the "up-down" liberation myth must be broken. Chinese feminism must stop confining itself within male-defined political fences. Feminists throughout the modern history of China, from or beyond the Party-state camp, need to be rediscovered and spread to build a feminist narrative of modern and contemporary China. This historical context is prominent in the current agenda of Weibo feminism.

Forgotten Armies of Women

She was born in 1871 to a wealthy and influential family in Hunan. As a child, she successfully resisted foot-binding. At 33, she began studying in Japan, where she met revolutionaries seeking to overthrow the Qing dynasty. Believing that the revolution could liberate Chinese women, she devoted herself to it, finally leading an army of 400 women to capture Nanjing, which became the capital of the newborn republic in 1912. However, male revolutionaries changed their rhetoric and refused to give women suffrage. After fruitless petitions and protesting, she and many other women rushed into and smashed the senate, slapping a male leader in the face. She strived for women's rights all her life. Her name is Tang Qunying (唐群英, 1871-1937).

Chinese feminism originated before the foundation of China's Communist Party (CCP). On Weibo, Luomeisheng (2020, 2021), a female history blogger, posted biographical articles on Tang Qunying alongside her contemporaries Zhang Zhujun (张竹君, 1876-1964) and Shen Peizhen (沈佩贞, ?-?) under the tag "Chinese Women's History." Just as their famous contemporary Qiu Jin (秋瑾, 1875-1907), all of them participated in the revolution of 1911 (a democratic revolution led by Dr. Sun Yat-sen that overthrew the Qing dynasty) and were the earliest awakening women or feminists in modern China. Their participation in the democratic revolution to overthrow the Qing Dynastic was built out of explicit and strong feminist intention: striving for equal rights for women and men, which they found expression in Sun Yat-sen's revolutionary agenda. Qiu Jin was killed by the Qing government in 1907, while the others realized the victory their peers had shed blood for betrayed their feminist appeals. Their fighting for women's suffrage in China echoed the transnational women's suffrage movement happening across the globe at the same time.

Young feminists on Weibo today are particularly interested in how these women fought alongside male revolutionaries but suffered betrayal, as male politicians of the Republic of China (1912–1949) broke their promise to endow women with suffrage immediately after they took power. Comparing revolutionaries of 1912 with the effacement and marginalization of female communists in the Communist Party and the underrepresentation of female medical workers in pandemic media coverage, a misogynistic coalition is revealed across political camps and times.

Another strategy to erase women's accomplishments, slut-shaming and slandering feminists, has been found throughout patriarchal history. A man the revolutionary Tang had never met claimed that Tang was his mistress and his story was published in a newspaper. Today, Weibo feminists are also slandered as madams, mistresses, or idle wives of high-level officers or even of U.S. diplomats, especially if they receive "foreign funds."

Feminism was taken over and then neglected in the communist camp, too. All-China Women's Federation was built nationally by integrating or annexing all existing women's organizations when the socialist government was established in 1949. Lu Lihua (陆礼华), a feminist activist and principal of a girls' school, had no choice but to see her school, career, and fortune taken over by the new government in 1950. Lu said she had no intention of organizing any women's association later, because this action would be considered as opposing the Women's Federation and therefore against the Party and the government (for which she could be punished). As for joining the Federation, she said: "The Women's Federation is not an organization you can join freely. Membership requires certain qualifications and has to be approved by different levels of authorities. In the end, you do not have initiative anymore" (Wang Z. 1999, 171). In recent years, Weibo feminists have shaken this monopoly on women's representation.

Instead of falling into the mental trap of figuring out to what degree the Party-state promoted women's rights and to what degree it hindered them, Weibo feminists focus on the work of female communists or socialists as individuals, independent of the Party. This method uncovers many new questions; for example, whether it is women who need the Party-state or the Party-state that needs women.

A feminist blogger quoted an online article about the large-scale discharge of all female soldiers before conferring formal military titles to all male members of the People's Liberation Army in 1955, following the end of the civil war and the establishment of the socialist government. The historical documents and practices mentioned are factual, although the article takes a conciliatory tone, attributing the discharge of female soldiers just before conferment to the adoption of the Soviet model, affirming that the female soldiers would be "the glory and pride of our army forever," even without military titles (Bingshuo 2020).

The feminist blogger underlined key facts from the article and made her own comments. There were approximately 110,000 female soldiers in the People's Liberation Army by the end of the "liberation" (civil war); 100,000 were discharged without honors—the terms of the official document are "settlement" (处理) or "retention" (留用) as "female workers" (妇女工作人员), rather than as female soldiers—while their male peers were triumphantly conferred formal military titles.

Calling this incident "the shame of the nation" (Wyujia 2020), the feminist blogger stressed the important role women played in the

revolution and protested the unjust distribution of power. She related it
to another famous misogynistic case in the Maoist age, "Eight-thousand
girls of Hunan to Mt. Tianshan." In the early 1950s, in order to settle the
area, the army stationed in Xinjiang Uygur Autonomous Region forced
thousands of eighteen-year-old girls to move there and marry soldiers.
The feminist blogger apparently believes the two incidents are
interrelated: women were first disarmed, then transported as national
goods. The inferior status of women is forged by the authorities. After
nearly two thousand reposts, the blogger's account was blocked.

The "women's liberation" or "equality between men and women"
defined by the Party-state and promoted by the Women's Federation
in the Maoist age often meant to embezzle female labor in a highly
exploitative way, while almost never granted women equal salaries
and treatments as males. For example, Iron Girl, the eulogized (also
masculinized) female socialist constructors in the Maoist age, resulted
from the shortage of male labors after war (Zhou and Guo 2013, 6; W.
Huang 2012). While women were encouraged to labor as "Iron Girl,"
shouldering as much, if not more, work as men, "equal payment for
equal work" has stayed as a watchword in most rural regions (Zhou
and Guo 2013, 7). "Iron Girl" was eulogized but never rewarded,
powerless in politics, even can't determine who to marry (8–9).

Women-friendly policies can be traced to communist or socialist
feminists in the margins of the male-dominated Party-state. The first
law published by the socialist government was the Marriage Law in
1950, drafted by seven female communists and led by Deng Yingchao
(邓颖超). As a senior communist revolutionary in the Party and wife
of the first premier Zhou Enlai (周恩来), Deng was among the
minority who persisted in advocating unconditional freedom for
divorce. Her speech at a meeting is recorded as follows:

> Why do I insist that divorce should be allowed as long as one side
> asks for it? Because China has been stuck in feudal society for a
> long time, with women the most oppressed. They suffered most

deeply in marriage. . . . The principle of allowing divorce when one side insists is primarily proposed for women's benefits. Adding extra conditions will just provide an excuse for officials with feudal thoughts to control and limit the freedom to divorce. In the past, we had no such principle, which caused many tragedies.[19]

But even the few achievements were lost in the reformation of later years and most recently the "cooling-off" period before divorce, which took effect in 2021. It fully illustrates that the Party-state is overturning what female communists such as Deng fought for. The Weibo account of *China Women's News* (2020), official media of the Women's Federation, posted to honor the 117th anniversary of Deng Yingchao's birth. The post had the tag, "She was a CCP member," instrumentalizing her contributions to glorify the Party. However, the first comment, with most "likes," is the quotation above, criticizing the current policy, followed by: "How shameless are you? How do you dare mention Deng Yingchao, while completely betraying her advocacy for freedom to divorce?" Women today are no longer falling for the trick of hijacking feminist contributions.

Feminist versions of China's modern history look different from the official accounts. Modern Chinese feminism began as a late nineteenth-century revolt against Confucian feudal patriarchy. Early feminists fought for women's civil rights, contributing to the modernization of China. They were constantly used and betrayed by the male revolutionaries they cooperated with. Today's Weibo feminists are skeptical of male-defined politics of both Chinese nationalism and Western liberalism and intent on expanding their own autonomous movement. They are faced with a masculinist superstructure rooted in Confucian times through the Maoist age to the post-reform era. Current researchers have described the superstructure as "a hybrid of socialist and Confucian patriarchy" (Ji et al. 2017, 768). How can feminists smash this patriarchal hybridity? Weibo feminists have some ideas.

Personal Revolts Change Politics

On February 12, 2021, the first day of the Chinese New Year, a man in Haining (Zhejiang province) stabbed his wife to death in the street. In China, it is said that what happens on the first day of the New Year will set the tone for the whole year, so that Chinese people try to make this the most joyful time possible. Whether the bloody first day of the new year will presage more atrocities against women remains to be seen, but similar cases have already been so recurrent as to numb public nerves. After the gradual close of the coronavirus response in the second half of 2020, news of women being murdered or fatally assaulted by intimate partners, family members, or even strangers are observed on Weibo almost every day. The crimes surpass ordinary domestic violence in bringing panic to the public because they are extremely violent and bloody and often took place in public places and neighborhoods, outside divorce registration offices or courts, and on the street. It is not merely intimate violence, but an open execution threatening women, in other words, femicide terrorism. With cases booming on social media, there must be many women who dare not refuse men's advances or propose breaking up or divorce, enduring violence without an escape. The reason for this surge may be the unbalanced gender ratio, which makes it hard for men to find wives, combined with the declining economy affected by the pandemic, causing frustrated men to get revenge on women.

The People's Daily (2019) has quoted a survey conducted by the All-China Women's Federation: 30 percent of the married women have suffered domestic violence. Women-hating terrorism is considered separately. A feminist then established "Evil Man" webpage recording hate crimes against women gathered from online news reports. Since 2016, it has assembled 1,876 total cases, of which 489 are assaults and murders of wives and girlfriends, not including 69 murders of entire families. The webpage was dedicated to "all surviving Chinese women" (cnwoman

2021). Such numbers are far from representing the actual statistics, which are not available in China, but all the separate cases gathered together reveal a systematic problem to the public, which is harder to ignore.

Why do these men kill or assault their partners? Although pretexts vary, we know for sure that murder is most often attempted when women are about to leave their abusers. The men would rather kill them than watch them go free. The murder mentioned above, according to information released by the police, happened when the killer drove from a distant city to Haining and caught his wife on the road (Qu 2021). In other words, the woman had probably been trying to leave her husband. In the 1950s, when women attempted to exert the divorce right guaranteed by the newly established Marriage Law, patriarchal families and institutions put up the strongest resistance possible; many women asking for divorce across the country were killed or tormented into suicide (H. Li 2008, 25–26).

Seeing these desperate revolts and violent retributions, no one could ever assume that marriage is only a personal affair. Getting married and divorced does happen on the individual level, but cases pile up that exhibit large-scale political conflicts around the marriage institution. The majority of those revolting against the institution are women, who made up 73.40 percent of the plaintiffs asking for divorce in court in 2016 and 2017, according to a report issued by China Justice Big Data Institute (CJBDI) in 2018. Those who want to maintain the institution are mostly men. What does marriage mean to men and women? How does it benefit men and disempower women? The answers to these questions can be found in the anti-marriage agenda of Weibo feminists.

Opposing Marriage Matters

Within the larger category of men, one group is most fervent about maintaining the marriage institution: the authorities. Only 34.19

percent of divorce petitions are granted by courts (CJBDI 2018). The juridical process can last for years. The "cooling-off" period before divorce, which took effect in 2021, will further delay the progress.[20] Domestic violence is rarely recognized by police and therefore cannot be cited in court. Killing a wife or girlfriend is subject to a lighter penalty than other murders, with a typical sentence of nine years in prison, often commuted (cnwoman 2021).

There is a deficit of marriageable women due to decades of selective abortion of female fetuses. Because of this and women's increased tendency to favor careers over marriage, the government launched a massive propaganda scheme to stigmatize women not married by their late 20s as lonely, pathetic "leftover women."[21] Women are pressured into marriage with little protection or means to escape male violence.

Weibo feminists consider marriage and the ensuing patriarchal family units a ruling mechanism. They campaign against the marriage institution and Confucian filial doctrines on a personal level to shake the existing injustice in laws and customs. Just as Lin Maomao (2021), now exiled from mainland China's cyberspace, remarked: "It is not that laws precede civil conditions; civil conditions precede laws."[22] When revolts from individuals through their personal lives accumulate, laws will be changed, and the politics will be changed.

Although online criticism can get personal in many emotional debates, major Weibo feminist bloggers clarify that they are against marriage as an institution and not against individuals who marry. Many married women also object to this institution, as it is common to realize the true nature of marriage after getting married. Opposing marriage does not mean reforming the marriage institution: "Expecting to find a good man to marry is no different from expecting a good ruler to maintain justice"[23] (Baiheihei and Shaoxi 2019). Marriage is inherently unfavorable and exploitative to women even when physical violence is not present. Refusing marriage is primarily a pragmatic choice for women's own benefits, in addition to the political aim to end patriarchy.

Weibo feminists analyze the marriage institution and its reformative forms. In talks about Chinese marriage, "bride price" or *cai li* (彩礼) has always been a heated topic. Traditionally, the male side provides bride price to initiate the handover of the woman from her father's family to her husband's family. Patriarchal families enslave each other's daughters by paying each other compensations for having raised the daughters.

Because of the unbalanced gender ratio and migration of women from rural areas to more female-friendly cities, millions of men in underdeveloped regions of China cannot find wives, and bride prices are high. Women in such regions are likely to be married at young ages to earn money for their families, especially for brothers to pay their own bride price, and are less likely to access education or employment in cities. For example, a 17-year-old girl in Guangxi was forced to marry a man she barely knew by her parents, who had also hidden her high-school admissions offer. The girl turned to the local authorities for help one day before the wedding. With media attention and action by the local authorities, the wedding was cancelled and the 50,000RMB (7,682 USD) bride price was refunded to the bridegroom's family (*The Paper* 2020). But such a resolute revolt against forced marriage is difficult for most teenage girls. They risk exclusion from families they depend on for survival, are threatened by domestic violence, and would need to set aside a lifetime of conditioning; and often they are not aware of their rights.

Turning a blind eye to the human rights violation of forced marriages, authorities typically resort to regulating bride price to provide affordable wives to working-class males. From the new Civil Law of 2021 to the first policy document of 2019 issued by the Central Committee of the CCP and the State Council (Xinhua News Agency 2019), the regulation of bride price is repeatedly stressed, while high dowry requirements, also common in some places, are never mentioned, though this could only worsen the gender ratio at birth in underdeveloped regions.

In most urban areas, couples no longer live with the male side's family, weakening the implication that women become their property. Men and women are expected to establish new small families through marriage. Modern, independent women equal to their husbands are not supposed to ask for bride price. Often both bride price and dowry become gifts from the parents to support the young couple. However, women are still obliged to bear offspring to continue their husbands' patriarchal ancestry, a basic forfeit of women's rights through marriage. (It is interesting to note that women in China do not take their husbands' surnames, though their children do.) Wives are also deprived of autonomy in sex, reproduction, abortion, and finances, subject to domestic violence, unpaid housework, attending to parents-in-law, and losing inheritance from their families of origin.

For some Weibo feminists, the only acceptable reformation of marriage would be to grant mothers' surnames to children. Only by changing marriage from an instrument to reproduce and control successors for patriarchal families can equality be envisioned. However, the significance of the surname issue lies more in exposing the lie of reformative marriage than in promoting the practice in reality. A Weibo feminist Enhe once commented on the picture of a successful online comedian holding her newborn baby that she looked exhausted, but her baby still bore her husband's surname. Such a simple remark with only dozens of reposts and responses was picked out as a target by many commercial accounts accusing extreme feminists of persecuting ordinary women. Millions of violent and insulting words were targeted at Enhe, who was herself, ironically, forbidden from posting (Laona 2020). The intentional anti-feminist revelry illustrates how firmly the core interest of the marriage institution is guarded.

Many Weibo feminists assert that they needn't strive for surname rights in marriage because they will never get married, while married women, if they do, only find their lives harder with husbands' families enraged. To tackle the core interest of patriarchal families from the inside will inevitably result in extreme retaliation. If marriage can't guarantee the core interest of patriarchy—ownership of offspring from wives' wombs and their additional unpaid labor—it is possible that male supremacists will oppose the marriage institution faster than feminists. The hegemony of marriage is also displayed in that unmarried women rearing children face difficulties accessing healthcare and registering their children, and same-sex unions are not recognized.

Therefore, Weibo feminists gave up their attempt to reform marriage but continue opposing it. Apart from being discriminated as "leftover women," marriage-resisters also forgo the only compensation patriarchy offers: sharing her husband's wealth and social resources. Patriarchal culture emphasizes this to intimidate and torment women: Not cooperating with men, you will have nothing. This reflects systemic inequality: "They robbed resources from you and required you to exchange a portion of what originally belonged to you with your womb. Wool comes from sheep, so how can sheep be winners?"[24] (Yingmianmian 2020).

A Weibo feminist tag sums up the alternative: "Plough your own field. You are a master; don't work as a tenant in the field of others."[25] Young women are encouraged to work hard, invest, buy themselves apartments, and accumulate their own fortunes staying away from marriage, and, when they are ready, bear children outside marriage.

Opposing Confucian Filial Obligations

In 2008, a group was established on Dou Ban, an online community in China, called "anti-parents"[26] (Nezumi 2017). Before it was blocked in

2017, the group had existed for almost ten years with more than 120,000 members, mostly teenagers or young adults sharing traumatic family experiences and anger toward manipulative parents. The group gave rise to much public attention and debate, as blaming and accusing parents is heretical in mainstream Chinese culture. The blocking of the group in 2017 coincided with the restoration of traditional norms by the authorities and the closure of a comparatively free age on the internet.

Most Chinese families are still dominated by Confucian norms. That parents provide more love and sacrifice than their offspring can ever repay is not to be questioned, nor that parents all have good intentions and love their children. However, beneath the myth of caring parents and filial children lies a deep unhappiness, especially among daughters. In 2021, a Weibo user posted a question: "What would you say if you could see your mom at 18 by time travel?" The three comments with the highest likes are: "Don't marry my father and don't give birth to me," "I hope Mom can continue her education—don't give up your future for anyone," and "Don't give birth to me; I don't like the world."

Confucian filial doctrine, as with marriage, is a fundamental ruling mechanism in China. It has no relation to love or any natural affection between individuals and is all about hierarchy, possessing human bodies, and conforming. In ancient times, parents could kill their children without being punished, while those who killed their parents (including parents-in-law for women) were subject to *lingchi*, a slow slicing execution torturing victims with thousands of cuts until death. Such a terrorizing penalty serves to uphold ruling principles. In the first policy document issued by the Central Committee of CCP and the State Council in 2019, "declination of filial doctrine" is listed under "bad social customs" to be punished (Xinhua News Agency, 2019). The ruling mechanism that has long been observed in Chinese families is once again ushered onto the stage of public policies.

Marriage is for reproduction, and reproduction is for raising and attending to parents. The reasons for restoring filial doctrine in the contemporary age include an aging population and encouraging childbirth to provide cheap labor and consumers. But most importantly, it serves to stabilize millions of surplus males with women and their children as nurturers and bearers of violence at the bottom of society. As feminists sharply point out, Chinese parents like urging their children to get married, because "offspring will be like their parents when they step onto the same road"[27] (Qingning 2021). If descendants don't enter marriage and become parents, they will not be turned into co-conspirators of the mechanism, upholding sacrificing parents and filial children.

In this intergenerational exploiting hierarchy, at the bottom are daughters. However, criticism of Confucian filial doctrines from the May Fourth Movement in 1919 revolves around the relationship between father and son. By using the terms "parents" (父母) or "offspring" (子女) to describe what is basically a father–son problem in the works of many male writers, daughters and mothers are ignored. When Fu Sinian (1896–1950) asks, "Do Chinese people create sons for their sons' sake?" and Hu Shi (1891–1962) laments, "I am not me, but only my parents' son,"[28] they take the specifically male position of sons (Q. Huang 2019, 25). Some female May Fourth writers did write about relationships between mothers and sons or mothers-in-law and daughters-in-law, but rarely about mother–daughter relationships (Dooling 2005).

An article by Lu Xun (1881–1936), "The Grave: How We Take the Role of Fathers Now"[29] directly illustrates the aim of the sons' revolts: to overthrow the pre-modern, persecuting and stubborn fathers and become reformative, modern, open-minded and benevolent fathers themselves. It was also the position held by the Communist Party when they advocated anti-feudalism, which included overthrowing all Confucian doctrines, during the revolutionary (1921–1949) and

Maoist (1949–1978) ages. However, the fathers inevitably turn into patriarchs, and the filial doctrines, never fully uprooted, are now emphasized to excuse unapologetically male rule.

Today's campaign on Weibo against Confucian filial doctrine is a daughters' revolt. Through the anti-marriage and autonomous reproduction outside marriage stance, they proudly claim that they will not "create patriarchs" (不造父). For the first time, this places "patriarchs" rightfully as something created by women rather than they being the creators. If women refuse to reproduce, or insist on doing so according to feminist terms, patriarchy cannot survive; the authorities are well aware of this.

Faced with awakened and revolting daughters, even the most powerful fathers find themselves in a powerless position. If the daughters want to, they can terminate the existence of patriarchy within a generation. Fathers have lost control of their daughters, but the complex mother–daughter emotional bond still grants manipulating power to mothers. Weak mothers caught in patriarchal families as hostages, and tough mothers defending filial doctrines as the families' guards, are weapons to deal with revolting daughters. The desire to save mothers draws daughters back from escaping or self-emancipation.

The systemic problem is answered by Weibo feminists through analyzing the alienation of motherhood by the patriarchal mechanism. When a mother gives birth to a baby in her husband's home, to bear her husband's surname, she deserts her baby immediately when the umbilical cord is cut. The baby is adopted by the patriarchal family and then, relying on her role as the father's wife, the mother reestablishes her relationship with the child. In other words, "All fathers in patriarchal families are adoptive fathers, all mothers are adoptive mothers, and all children are orphans"[30] (Yangxinshu 2019). The emotional exploitation of daughters by mothers is also illustrated:

I am the daughter at the bottom of my family, never taken seriously or loved. But a child can push me up. Stepping on the top of my child, I will never fall to the bottom again.

Rear a child, then the child is my savor from a sea of bitterness. She/he becomes . . . an object I squeeze love and care from. What's more, the social culture and laws force her/him to show no regrets, incapable of complaining and blaming.[31]

Baobaolie 2021

In this struggle between revolting daughters and mothers defending filial doctrine, criticism toward mothers from Weibo feminists is often mistakenly blamed as attacking women. On the contrary, it is an attempt to emancipate women from the mother–daughter relationship that is distorted by patriarchy. Lin Maomao is renowned for expressing her ideas with sharp, ironic, and comic language. As a mother of two daughters, she remorselessly comments that the "hostage mothers" are not innocent, but foremost partners of the fathers: "Those who sleep in the same bed are of the same type." She asserts that her position as a mother enables her to tell daughters the truth: "Their mothers don't love kids, or they wouldn't marry the pig-headed fathers, rearing ugly children single-handedly, causing overpopulation and fierce social competition."[32]

Weibo feminists not only advocate that young women refuse financial and emotional exploitation from their families but also encourage them to strive for inheritance rights. Men have an edge in access to financial support from families, while women are left to themselves, even when they are only children. One feminist warns other women with her own example. While she strove to save money in the most difficult period of her life to prove her ability to her parents, her father lent large sums to relatives who assumed they were justified in taking a sonless family's fortune (Huoxu 2021b). This woman was determined to take over her father's business. Daughters should not be shy in asking for the financial support from parents that sons automatically receive. No matter how much they get, the most important thing is to consider themselves as heirs of their families.

Reflecting on what caused her to be blocked from China's entire cyberspace, Lin Maomao said that she only made two points through her posts: "First, women, you have reproduction rights and can determine who you bear; second, women, you have inheritance rights and can decide who you love."[33] This also summarizes the current agenda of Weibo feminism against marriage and Confucian filial obligations.

Most importantly, Weibo feminists encourage women to take action for themselves and refuse, resist, and disobey, which is probably the main reason it is viewed as a threat by the authorities. They are active self-empowering advocates for women. As Lilylinmu (2021) posted: "You don't need the country to abolish marriage, patriarchal surnames, visiting (in-laws') homes during the Chinese New Year. You only need not to participate yourself, then to you, they are abolished."[34]

In face of high-handed censorship and other risks, and neglected by academia, Weibo feminists believe in the value of their work. Through spreading feminist theories and agendas online, they awaken one individual after another, a force they believe will eventually overpower the patriarchal mechanism: "To eliminate patriarchy, shaking the established values while creating new ones is not only enough, but perhaps the most effective way for transformation"[35] (Baiheihei 2019). After all, society is formed by the people.

Works Cited

Baiheihei [@白黑黑] & Shaoxi [@稍息-shaoxi]. (2019, February 9). 当我们说反婚，我们是在说些什么 [What We Talking When We Advocate Anti-Marriage].
Weibo. https://m.weibo.cn/1370505990/4337805569873608.

Baiheihei [@白黑黑]. (2019, June 15). 社会秩序如何成为可能 [How Social Order Forms]. Weibo. https://m.weibo.cn/1370505990/4383301588936822

Baobaolie [@暴暴烈甜心小鳄鱼毛毛]. (2021, February 10). 做母亲生孩子，在等国对于多数女性来说都是巨大的诱惑 [For Most Women in China, Rearing Children to Be Mother Is a Great Temptation]. Weibo. https://m.weibo.cn/6504596840/4602978792903431.

Bingshuo [兵说]. (2020, February 14). 1955年授衔，谁的意见最大？并非"李云龙"，10万女兵集体退役，原因竟跟苏联有关 [Military Titles Conferring in 1955: 100,000 Female Soldiers Took off Their Uniforms]. Sohu. http://3g.k.sohu.com/t/n426144813?showType=&sf_a=weixin&from=groupmessage.

Chen, H. (2021, January 23). 如果穿越见到18岁的妈妈，你会对她说什么 [What Would You Say to Your Mom If You Met her at her Eighteen by Time Travel]. Weibo. https://m.weibo.cn/1792995502/4596650364118524.

Chen, J. (2016). 早期婚姻伦理文化与商代女性 [Preliminary Marriage Ethic and Culture and Women in Shang Dynasty]. *Shandong Social Science*, 6, 510–511.

ChuanA [@川A1234567]. (2021, March 21). 三星堆是外星文明吗 [Is Sanxingdui Alien Civilization]. Weibo. https://m.weibo.cn/7513210373/4617210423413035.

China Women's News [@中国妇女报]. (2021, February 4). 中国妇女运动的蓬勃开展，离不开这位伟大的女性 [The Thriving of Chinese Feminist Movement Is Bound with This Great Woman]. Weibo. https://m.weibo.cn/2606218210/4600975844980342.

CJBDI. (2018). 司法大数据专题报告之离婚纠纷(2016-2017) [The Juridical Bigdata Report: Divorce Cases]. China Justice Big Data Service Platform. Beijing: CJBDI. http://data.court.gov.cn/pages/uploadDetails.html?keyword=司法大数据专题报告之离婚纠纷(2016-2017).pdf.

cnwoman. (2021, February 08). *Evil Man*. Github: cnwoman-bot.github.io/evil-man/

Daode [@道德绝世小]. (2021, January 27). 所以周推翻商，到底是谁得利了 [So who benefit from Zhou dynasty's overthrowing of Shang]. Weibo. https://m.weibo.cn/2468217705/4597937218526479.

Dooling, Amy. *Writing Women in Modern China: The Revolutionary Years, 1936–1976*. Columbia UP.

Hong Fincher, L. (2018). *Betraying Big Brother: The Feminist Awakening in China.* London & New York: Verso.

Hongli [@红鲤蛆与绿鲤蛆和驴]. (2019, November 5). *且父母之于子也，产男则相贺，产女则杀之* [People Celebrate the Birth of Sons, and Kill Newborns If They are Daughters.]. Weibo. https://m.weibo.cn/7157921721/4435409787982205.

Huang, C. (2011). *中国婚姻调查* [Investigation of Chinese Marriage]. Beijing: The Writers Publishing House.

Huang, Q. (2019). The Paradox of Filial Piety in the Period of the May Fourth Movement. *Literature, History and Philosophy* (3), 24–34.

Huang, Wei. (2012). *文革时期女性形象政治化研究* [The Politicalization of Female Image during the Culture Revolution]. Shoudu Normal University, 2012.

Huoxu[@或许不如不见]. (2021, February 11). *继承权这个事情，凭什么女孩子不能提* [Why Can't Daughters Put forward the Issue of Inheritance]. Weibo. https://m.weibo.cn/3524285233/4603249493279017.

Ji, Y., Wu, X., Sun, S., and He, G. (2017). Unequal Care, Unequal Work: Toward a more Comprehensive Understanding of Gender Inequality in Post-reform Urban China. *Sex Roles* (77), 765–778.

Laona [@老衲很欣慰]. (2020, May 12). *转发豆瓣* [Repost from Douban]. Weibo. https://m.weibo.cn/status/4503776595132507?.

Li, W. (2017). *"红颜祸水"论源于周人对商代的女性文化否定* [The Myth of "Beautiful Women Cause a Kingdom Collapse" Originated from the Zhou's Negation of Feminist Culture of Shang Dynasty]. *Journal of Foshan University (Social Science)*, 35(5), 18–23.

Li, H. (2008). Family/Marriage-related Death of Women at the Beginning of Liberation. *Collection of Women's Studies* (3), 24–30.

Lilylinmu [@Lily林mu]. (2020, July 30). *耕自己的地，你本是地主，不要去别人地里当长工* [Plough your own field. You are a master; don't work as a tenant in the field of others]. Weibo. https://m.weibo.cn/7484401377/4532431011717444

Lilylinmu [@Lily林mu]. (2021, February 13). *总有人说"如果取消XX就好了"* [There're Always People Saying: "What if . . . Is Abolished"]. Weibo. https://m.weibo.cn/7484401377/4604163189382844

Luo, S. (2017). 离婚冷静期: 家事审判方式改革的重大举措——评四川安岳法院签发的首份《离婚冷静期通知书》 [Calming Down Period the Vital Reform in the Judgement of Domestic Affairs: Comments on the First Calming Down Order Issued by the Court of Anyue, Sichuan Province]. *Democracy and Legal System*, (13), 48–49.

Luomeisheng [@洛梅笙]. (2020, November 22). 王贞仪在死之前 [Before Wang Zhenyi's Death]. Weibo. https://m.weibo.cn/2034280670/4574197764331312.

Luomeisheng [@洛梅笙]. (2021, January 2). 说到中国近代以来争取将男女平等写入宪法 [Talking about Putting Women's Equal Status into the Constitute in Modern China]. Weibo. https://m.weibo.cn/2034280670/4589004895294384.

Nezumi. (2017, December 29). "父母皆祸害" 小组10年考 [A Summary Study of the Team "All Parents Are the Source of Misfortune" at its Tenth Anniversary]. Douban: douban.com/note/651021705/.

Qingning [@青柠甜莓]. (2021, February 13). Weibo. https://m.weibo.cn/2833159894/4604254084662277.

Qu, C. (2021, February 12). 浙江海宁一男子大年初一杀死妻子 已被警方控制 [A Men Killed His Wife on the First Day of the New Year and Has Been Controlled by the Police]. *Beiqing News*. xw.qq.com/partner/vivoscreen/20210212A05RWR00?pgv_ref=vivoscreen&ivk_sa=1023197a

Shangshen [@舨深之渊]. (2020, January 27). 父亲卖女为娼 [Father Sold Daughter as Whore]. Weibo. https://m.weibo.cn/1918121730/4597935118230483.

Shuangla [@爽辣冷人]. (2021, January 26). 圣杯与剑2 [The Chalice and the Blade, Video 2]. Weibo. . https://m.weibo.cn/2429512484/4597678959232649.

The Paper News. (2020, June 29). 17岁少女举报被爸妈逼婚嫁给邻村男子，错过上高中 [A Seventeen-year Old Girl Reported Her Parents Forcing Her to Get Married out of High School]. Weibo. https://weibo.com/ttarticle/x/m/show/id/2309354521133759136000?_wb_client_=1.

The People's Daily. (2019, November 27). 你怎么看家暴只有0次和无数次 [Domestic Violence Never Happens Just Once]. Weibo. https://weibo.com/2803301701/Ii6QSzvv6?type=comment.

Wang, S. (2020). 王阳明六经"删述"说发微——兼论文化生态的净化 [Historical Probe of WANG Yangming's Ethical Explanation of Confucian Deletion and Compilation of Six Classics from Perspective of Purification of Cultural Eco-system]. *Journal of Hubei University (Philosophy and Social Science)*, 47(5), 85–93.

Wang, K. (2019). "Ching I Sao in Fact and Fiction." *Comparative Literature and Transcultural Studies*, 3(1), 82–95.

Wang, Z. (1999). *Women in the Chinese Enlightenment: Oral and Textual Histories.* University of California Press.

Wesoky, S. R. (2016). Politics at the Local-Global Intersection: Meanings of Bentuhua and Transnational feminism in China. *Asian Studies Review*, 40(1), 53–69.

Wuming [@物鸣的垃圾箱]. (2021, February 14). 女人与家国情怀 [Women and National Emotional Bound]. Weibo. m.weibo.cn/1111790250/4604496422111719

Wyujia [@W瑜伽无人认领]. (2020, November 5). 突然账号异常 [My Account Turned Abnormal Suddenly]. Weibo. https://m.weibo.cn/1800751037/4545802607002992

Xiao, X. and Wu W. (2010). 三星堆遗址仁胜村土坑墓出土玉石器初步研究 [A Preliminary Study of Jade and Stone Items from Tombs of Rensheng Village in Sanxingdui Site]. Sichuan Cultural Relics, 2, 33–43.

Xinhua News Agency. (2019, February 19). 中共中央国务院关于坚持农业农村优先发展做好"三农"工作的若干意见 [Some Ideas on Prioritizing Development of Agriculture and Rural Areas for the Accomplishment of Work in Agriculture, Rural Areas and Rural Dwellers from Central Commmission of Communist Party, China and the State Council]. Government of China: www.gov.cn/zhengce/2019-02/19/content_5366917.htm.

Yangxinshu [@yangxinshu]. (2019, March 5). 母缘断裂 [The Breaking-up of Mother-Child Bound]. Weibo. https://m.weibo.cn/1759932171/4346427037235054.

Yeqingcheng [@作家叶倾城]. 中国第一代女留学生中 [Among the First Generation of Chinese Females Studying Abroad]. Weibo. https://m.weibo.cn/1182419985/4619691731456544.

Yingmianmian [@硬晚晚]. (2020, Decmber 7). *其实婚姻的机制很简单* [The Mechanism of Marriage Is Quite Simple]. Weibo. https://m.weibo.cn/6512113818/4579587667272013.

Zhao, M. (2018). *孔子"删诗"说的来源与产生背景* [The Origin and Background of the Sayings of "Confucius Delecting Poems"]. *Confucius Studies*, 5, 22–30.

Zhou, D. and Guo Y. (2013). "Gender, Power and Identity Construction --- Taking Dazhai's 'Iron Girls' as a Case." Nationalities Research in Qinghai, 24(1), 5–10.

Zuo, C. and Yang W. (2017). *"殷周革命"中女性贵族等级身份的变迁* [Changing Status in the Hierarchal Soceity of Aristocratic Women during Zhou Replacing Shang]. *Ningxia Social Science*, 1, 191–196.

3

Hijacking Reproductive Rights

In 2019, the American documentary *One Child Nation* turned the focus once again to China's one-child policy, although it had already ended in 2015. Made by two Chinese women born under the policy, the film explores the impact from various sides and includes voices of local officials responsible for enforcing it and doctors required to perform abortions. Many have wondered why this policy, instituted in 1978, lasted 38 years without any significant resistance. This documentary suggests that resistance was impossible due to the privation of individual autonomy under the pressure of an authoritarian mechanism. This view negates the essential contribution of people's cooperation.

Saying that the people were cooperative might seem callous when the film shows houses being torn down and cattle dragged away for those who did not comply. But the officials punishing those who transgressed were also subject to the policy. Overall, daughter-only families were the most determined to revolt, in order to have sons. Rural families already secured with sons, by chance or selective abortion, or urban workers in public enterprises on the state payroll, kept silent. Attributing the policy's success to tyrannical rulers only alienates it from the many similar laws and customs that instrumentalize women's bodies as tools of reproduction.

The one-child policy is an extreme example, but far from unique. Reproductive control fits into a cultural and political ethic that is not specific to one time or place. In China, encouraging childbirth dates back to ancient times and was prevalent in the 1950s–1960s. In ancient times, parents were punished if they didn't send their daughters to be married after a certain age, which was usually between fifteen and seventeen.[1] In the Han Dynasty (202 B.C–220 A.D.), an emperor ordered that unmarried women over fifteen be required to pay five times more taxes.[2] In the early 1950s, abortions and contraception were illegal in China (Jin 2015). Today, many women report online that they are required to prove consent from husbands or partners when seeking abortions in hospitals (Xunxunzi 2021).

Although violating women's rights to make decisions about their bodies has been widespread throughout the male-dominated world, it has never drawn so much attention as it has with the one-child policy. When encouraging childbirth, driving women into marriage, and limiting abortion rights, China's national will was unquestioned, as it was consistent with the interests of patriarchal families and males. Only in the case of the one-child policy did nationalism and patriarchy clash, with women's bodies caught in the middle. The one-child policy is cited, especially in the West, as a violation of human rights, while reproductive control before and after are not.

Meanwhile, research focuses on the imbalance in sex ratio in China during the one-child policy, implying that the policy is the primary cause for sex-selective abortion and the deserting or killing of female babies. History and recent statistics suggest otherwise. According to the National Bureau of Statistics (2020), in a survey conducted in 2019, the male–female ratio among children aged 0 to 4 (that is, all born after the end of the one-child policy in 2015) is 113.62. This shows only a slight decline and an imbalance that is still the world's most severe. There is not necessarily a correlation, as the sex ratio at birth was most severe in 2005 and began declining thereafter (Sobotka and Zhang 2019). In 2017, after the end of the one-child policy, the sex ratio at the second birth is 109, while for the third birth it rises to 138. This suggests that the end of the one-child policy might save a portion of first-born girls, but sex-selective abortion for the second or third births is still rampant. Research on the sex ratio at birth in the 1970s before the implement of the one-child policy shows that in certain groups, severe sex ratio imbalance had already emerged (Babiarz et al. 2009). Before the one-child policy and accessible abortions, the missing girls were not unregistered or aborted as fetuses; they were killed after birth.

Before and after the one-child policy, the supposed reproductive freedom usually meant coercing or forcing women to deliver children, and patriarchal families were not willing to rear girls. Abandoning and killing female babies has been recorded as early as the third century B.C. in *Han Fei Zi*: "Sons born, people congratulate one another, and daughters born are to be killed."[3] Historian Michelle King (2014) has also traced the deep roots of female infanticide in China. Where abortion is available, selective procedures replace deserting or killing girls after birth. It is illegal for doctors to reveal a fetus' sex, but this is easy to circumvent.

The authoritarian one-child policy is conveniently framed as the killer, concealing the true culprits: patriarchal and patrilineal family norms and the exploitative parent–offspring contract issued by Confucian filial doctrine. The problem is rooted in women's loss of reproductive autonomy for the past several thousand years, and this is the primary reason the extreme one-child policy was possible.

The policy fits seamlessly into China's historical, cultural, and political constructs. The government regulates the population's reproduction just as parents (patriarchs) determine the life and death of their offspring under the Confucian filial doctrines. This includes millennia of femicide. The ideology behind the policy and the ongoing patriarchal tradition are identical. People will not completely go against a policy whose foundations they believe in, even if they attempt to evade it to guarantee that their own families are not among those sacrificed with no sons.

This is why the topic of reproduction is so important that Chinese feminists on Weibo must address it in their daily feminist output. The end of the one-child policy indicates the resolution of struggles between patriarchal authorities and patriarchal families. Now, with the conspiracy of both, public and private violation of women's reproduction rights take on new exploitative methods through technologies such as surrogacy. Although Weibo feminists analyze the end of the one-child policy in different lights, they find common ground in their criticism of surrogacy. They do not, as do many liberal feminists in the West, consider this an issue of a woman's choice in what to do with her own body. They highlight the ways in which such "choices" related to reproduction are rarely free of coercion, misinformation, and exploitation. They urge women to reclaim their autonomy in reproduction through self-empowerment as the only way to terminate controlling policies of all kinds.

The Only Daughter's Dilemma

While Weibo feminists agree that the one-child policy's practices of forced abortions and unconsented contraceptive implants after birth were cruel violations of female bodies, some have viewed the one-child policy as an antidote to patriarchal family control. Traditionally, women were required to bear many children, placing more burdens on them than one child. Some argue that interference from the authorities limited the exploitation of female bodies by patriarchal families, increasing their participation in the workforce. In addition, the policy created a large quantity of only daughters, unlikely to happen otherwise in Chinese culture. These only daughters enjoy the allocation of attention and resources traditionally given only to sons. Many only daughters cite this side effect of the policy, which was certainly not among the authorities' intentions (Yangguang 2021).

Many other feminists oppose such views and emphasize the historical and cultural context of controlling women's bodies that the policy has furthered. Even if some individual women benefited from it, the policy is profoundly misogynistic and thus inimical to long-term and deep-rooted social change. While critical of the only-child policy, they are more interested in the government's current strategy of encouraging childbirth, to which the policy, as we will see, is linked.

Whether they consider themselves lucky to have been born under the one-child policy or pity their mothers, those who feel guilty about their only-child identity are the only daughters, not sons. The "dilemma of only daughters" is a by-product of the policy that has been ignored by researchers. The unique only-daughter experience expounds the government's current difficulty in coercing women into producing more offspring to relieve an aging population.

Some researchers have suggested that only daughters are subject to the same high expectations and investment of enormous resources for education, etc. as sons, and that this enables them to be more sensitive to, and revolt against, gender inequality in the public space (Q. Wang 2018). Though there may be some truth to this, most only daughters have not grown into feminists. The difficulties and dilemmas they face are far more complicated than this optimistic portrayal.

In terms of family investment and inheritance rights, only daughters have not won an equal place with sons. According to traditional beliefs, the only advantage of raising a daughter is that it saves a lot of money, as families with boys are obliged to buy or build new residences and pay the bride price for sons when they marry, as well as investing in their education and professional training, while daughters are expected to move into their future husbands' homes. Although in big cities, the housing loan is often paid after marriage and the bride's family also invests in the new residence by providing renovation, women's names are included on the deeds of only 30 percent of marital homes (Hong Fincher 2014, 46). In rural areas, women are mostly deprived of the rights to access curtilages, distributed to families with grown sons from the public-owned land of villages (H. Li 2017, 57). Therefore, Chinese women "were shut out of the biggest accumulation of real-estate wealth in history" (Hong Fincher, 2014, 44).

Weibo feminists share struggles for inheritance rights. One woman, having no brothers, assumed that the family fortune from her parents' business would fall to her and her younger sister. However, after attending universities and then working outside her hometown for years, she found out that male relatives had been eroding her family fortune by borrowing money from her father and buying shares of the family business, while her father had been cultivating this male alliance: "Seeing our family has no son, the relatives plan to eat up our fortune without an heir, because they all tacitly assume that daughters have no inheritance rights. After I get married, my parents' fortune has nothing to do with me."[4] Now she has moved back home to inherit her family business and sued the relatives.

Chi jue hu (吃绝户), literally meaning eating up families without male heirs, is considered a phenomenon from traditional or underdeveloped regions in China, where families with only daughters are subject to discrimination, bullying, and robbery of their fortunes and lands. However, even to most urban only daughters, marriage has never been equal, and conservativism (inequality) is increasing and spreading today. Only daughters living in homes owned by their husbands and giving birth to children bearing their husbands' family names, although they might receive support from parents who have no other children, still feel annexed or consumed unless they create new family and child-nurturing patterns as feminists. This is a prominent goal of Weibo feminism today.

Only daughters may enjoy treatment similar to sons within their families but not similar social standing. The core of patriarchal marriage is the wife's obligation to continue her husband's familial line, and only daughters do not escape this exploitation. Through the male-benefitting marriage institution, the only daughter's family fortune will also be diverted into the pockets of their husbands' families. The unprecedented number of only daughters has not changed the marriage institution. Instead, larger numbers of women than ever before choose to remain single. However, staying single goes against traditional norms and usually cannot be accepted by their families. When families lose their only daughters through marriage, they may become critical of certain practices, yet do not go to the root of the problem, still unconcerned with thousands of years of gynocidal tradition and female erasure. Apart from forcing their daughters to get married, many such families mend their loss by deepening the exploitation of women, as we will see.

A new pattern of "two-sided marriage" (两头婚) is prevailing in some rich villages in southeastern coastal provinces. A couple marries with neither bride price nor dowry and live separately with their own families most of the time. The woman delivers two children, one under the husband's surname and one under her own (Zhao and Fan 2020).

Contrary to some media that consider this new marriage custom progressive and egalitarian, Weibo feminists remark: "Taking out two hundred yuan from the wife's pocket to allocate one hundred to each side, you call this gender equality?"[5] By forcing women to rear two children and give one away to another family for free, patriarchal families with only daughters trade back the right to obtain offspring. The only daughters are still traded, just as others are married off to gain bride price for their brothers.

One participant in a pregnant women's chat room related that she was an only daughter pregnant as a surrogate mother for her parents. After graduating high school, she became a surrogate mother because her parents wanted to have a son (Yili 2021). Such examples highlight discrepancies in what benefits only daughters and what benefits their parents and how patriarchal families "mend their loss" by further exploiting their only daughters.

Injustice in Public Policies: The Hegemony of Patriarchy

Women's rights to control their own bodies are carved up by patriarchal institutions. Women are required to cede reproductive control to men as decision-makers in public and private. Gaining offspring through controlling women or "colonizing" their bodies and minds is the fundamental privilege of men in patriarchal families. This is perhaps most apparent in the punishment of women who give birth without being married to a man.

Though the authorities encourage childbirth, single women are not allowed to buy sperm or freeze their eggs for themselves. The only systemic relic of the one-child policy is the systematic punishment of women rearing children outside the heterosexual marriage institution. Even when they have stable jobs with insurance that would normally cover pregnancy and birth, unmarried women must pay all medical expenses. As punishment for their single status, they also cannot access paid maternity leave with guaranteed job retention as can married mothers in China. A single mother in Shanghai demanded her rights for four years before finally receiving insurance payments (Sohu News 2021). The authorities didn't leave much time for women to celebrate it. After a few months, it was found that to apply for the insurance online, the ID number of the husband must be input. Still, single mothers may be required to pay a fine to declare a birth. Fines for "reproduction outside the plan" (计划外生育), a relic of the one-child policy, now only applies to single mothers. Fines are demanded whether the woman chose to have a child on her own or was abandoned by the child's father, sending a message to all women that their survival and that of any offspring depends on a man's approval. It also suggests that, even though the government wants more births, their first priority is ensuring the continuation of patriarchal control.

These policies highlight that what the authorities are encouraging is in fact only childbirth within the marriage institution. Only the population under the control of the patriarchal mechanism is considered desirable to increase. Social welfare granted to patriarchal units instead of to women who rear children is an award for males who manage to control women and can upgrade themselves to the status of patriarchs.

Similarly, in terms of custody, the authorities assist patriarchal families in tearing children away from their mothers. The court usually supports patrilineal families' claims for custody in divorce cases. In the Weibo super-chat Purple-Ribbon Mother, mothers who lost custody of small children appeal to the public for action. Many had children forcefully removed by ex-husbands' families and were never allowed to see them again. In the single mother Wei Yuanyuan's case, giving birth to a son unmarried, she was required, by a court in Beijing, not only to hand her infant to her ex-boyfriend's family, but also to pay them child support of thousands of yuan per month. Here, the hegemony of patriarchy expands beyond the marriage institution.

In another case, a woman gave birth to a baby through in-vitro fertilization with a donor's sperm, as her husband was infertile. Two years later, when she proposed divorce, her husband's family kidnapped her son from her home. Though the man is neither the biological father nor has ever cared for the baby, courts still ruled in his favor. This case makes it clear that family names, not biological or social realities, are the pretext for appropriating women's bodies and resultant children. The only consistency is male supremacy and maintenance of patriarchal lineage, which the government views as the best insurance of "social stability"—the unquestioned continuance of its rule. Men will not mind being oppressed by the government as long as there is someone lower in status who they can exploit (or as long as men are granted "subhumans" as Weibo sci-fi puts it). The human rights and welfare of women and children come last.

Assisted reproductive technology (ART) often works to further exploit women's bodies, enabling men without viable sperm to have offspring by putting wives through the painful process of egg retrieval and in-vitro fertilization and health risks of miscarriages. With the decline of the one-child policy, the hijacking of women's reproductive rights intensifies, especially in collaboration with modern biological technology with the threat of commercial surrogacy becoming legal in China. Weibo feminists have launched perhaps their largest online protest, clashing with "public opinion" generated by the authorities.

A Unified Anti-surrogacy Stance

Opposing all forms of surrogacy is the shared objective of Weibo feminists. They are unprecedentedly united and highly sensitive to this topic, sparing no efforts to popularize relevant knowledge and criticism, taking an active part in resisting the probe of the authorities and commercial surrogacy businesses. These efforts have brought surrogacy to public attention. The anti-surrogacy campaign of Weibo feminists is the largest obstacle to the government's aim to legalize surrogacy.

Why are feminists on Weibo so concerned with surrogacy? The tags they have created include, "Against surrogacy in all forms" and "Oppose surrogacy or head to hell." Does such rhetoric overestimate the importance of the issue? Confronting an overwhelming force consisting of the tacit support of the authorities, profit-chasing capitalism, and a culture thirsty for filial sons, Weibo feminists realize that women are at high risk. If surrogacy, even in its "altruistic" (without declared payment) form, is legalized, millions of Chinese women will fall into the abyss.

From changes in laws and articles, an attempt to promote the legalization of surrogacy is detected, while the already existing underground surrogacy centers and reckless advertisements for overseas surrogacy imply that danger has already come to the door. A significant portion of surrogacy customers in California travel from mainland China and are not criminalized. Weibo feminists call attention to the disastrous consequences of surrogacy and the risks it represents for every Chinese woman.

Facing criticism from both government-sponsored media and U.S.-influenced liberalism, Weibo feminists stand strong and united. The U.S. is unlike most developed countries, where surrogacy is banned and considered a human rights violation revolving around gender and class. Instead, it is legal in many U.S. states. Erasing surrogate mothers (including through altruistic stereotypes), the U.S. media depicts surrogacy in a rosy glow and even frames it as a gay rights issue. Many Chinese intellectuals are influenced by the U.S., and in this case the viewpoint corresponds with China's government's own leanings.

According to Weibo feminists, the liberal LGBTQ movement, popular in the West and gaining momentum in China, does not get to the roots of patriarchy and might even be another front for men's interests. As one Weibo feminist put it, "Is our goal to broaden the territory ruled by patriarchal gender morality and norms or overthrow it completely?"[6] (Mew 2018). This does not signify that Weibo feminists are against homosexuality, and the movement includes many lesbians. Rather, they cite how homosexual men, as men, still benefit from cultural privileges placing their interests above those of lesbians and all women. Overtly granting certain rights to gay men at the expense of women is "broadening the territory" of patriarchy in China today. Certain "advances" help patriarchal institutions expand and transform. Highlighting the economic interests at stake, they consider surrogacy an example of this.

In a Delicate Suspension: Legal Gray Areas

Surrogacy in all forms is declared to be illegal in China by government-sponsored media, but this is more to assuage public objections than to enforce any restrictions. Preparation to legalize commercial surrogacy began in 2015 when the term prohibiting surrogacy in any forms was deleted from the Amendment of Population and Family Planning Law (人口和计划生育法). This is in tune with the national policy to encourage childbirth and also meet the demand of the upper classes to have offspring, especially sons, more conveniently. An online anti-surrogacy outbreak followed and has continued to the present day. In response, some official media expressed their "steadfast" stance against commercial surrogacy. Meanwhile, the government continues to turn a blind eye to the already existing commercial surrogacy business in both China and for Chinese couples who travel overseas. The prohibition of surrogacy remains only in Technical Regulation of Assisted Reproductive Technology (人工辅助生殖管理办法), a document issued by the National Heath Commission in 2003, which doesn't mention any punishment (Shi 2015; C. Wang 2015).

In 2017, the government-controlled *People's Daily* stated: "Nearly 90% of women over 45 are infertile, and doctors suggest allowing surrogacy in proper ways" (J. Wang 2017). Reversing feminist concerns over increased exploitation of women's bodies (especially poor women), surrogacy is framed as actually responding to women's need. This message, essentially testing the waters, received tens of thousands of objections on Weibo before it was deleted.[7]

Despite the government's insistence that commercial surrogacy is illegal in China, the law specifies no punishment for it. Surrogacy businesses openly advertise on digital mass media and elsewhere. Surrogacy is actually already legalized, just without the open acknowledgement of authorities. In early 2021, the surrogacy scandal of a famous Chinese actress Zheng Shuang (郑爽), accused of abandoning two children born from U.S.-based surrogate mothers, exposes dark secrets of the Chinese upper class. The authorities responded by strictly prohibiting the actress from speaking to the public (P. Zhang 2021).

Meanwhile, a feminist on Weibo discovered that Suzhou Basecare Medicine, a mainland Chinese company providing ART (assisted reproductive technology) was coveted by the major investment firm Hillhouse Capital, which is considered a bad sign (Heiye 2021). As Weibo feminists predicted, the market has already decided that assisted reproduction in China will be a booming industry.

In addition to surrogacy centers and companies in China (in a legal gray area), advertisements for surrogacy in foreign countries are also common online. A feminist on Weibo reposted a surrogacy advertisement exhibiting dozens of pictures of beautiful "egg girls" (卵妹) (young women said to be egg providers) and surrogate mothers. They are advertised openly as high-quality goods to quickly purchase, with comments on their physical characteristics such as shining skin, big eyes, body shape, good health, and young age (Chuan 2021a). This type of advertisement has even been found right under the news that a baby girl was deserted by the intended parents and adopted by the surrogate mother (Chuan 2021b). Website advertisements are often thrown in the most relevant webpages or IP addresses by computer algorithms, which means surrogacy advertisements run freely in highly censored Chinese cyberspace. (The same is true of pornography, technically illegal but ubiquitous.)

The authorities refuse to acknowledge that the commercial surrogacy industry is already taking off. *China Women's News*, the official publication of the All-China Women's Federation, provides a glimpse of the Party-state's stance on the topic. Generally speaking, *China Women's News* stresses the potential risks of commercial surrogacy and its illegality. But its stance can be contradictory and changeable, showing that the Federation is in the margins of the ruling mechanism, unable to hold its own opinion and is most often used as a tool to assuage public emotions.

In 2015, the year "prohibiting surrogacy in all forms"[8] was deleted from the law, one article introduced the proposal of a representative of the People's Congress, that laws should be set to regulate surrogacy; this means an overt legalization of it. The article states: "Surrogacy serves to honor the reproductive rights of infertile couples" (C. Wang, 2015). After 2017, when Weibo feminists had successfully swayed public opinion, there was official content vowing to "continue to harshly forbid surrogacy that is against law and regulations" (Geng 2017). However, the agency to "harshly forbid" is the National Health Commission, which has no judicial penalizing power. In principle, as long as a surrogacy institution doesn't assert itself as a hospital-like medical unit, it would be out of the jurisdiction of the Commission. In 2021, when the anti-surrogacy voice prevailed in the Chinese digital world, an article in *China Women's News* proposed adding commercial surrogacy as a crime in the penal code (H. Zhang 2021).

However, when news exposed that a girl born in a China-based surrogacy center was deserted by the buyer, and her surrogate mother who adopted her was unable to get the child registered for school, *China Women's News* appealed to the biological parents to assist with the child's registration (L. Li 2021), downplaying the injustice. In actress Zheng Shuang's surrogacy scandal, *China Women's News* argued that abandoning children was a different issue from commercial surrogacy (Y. Yang and H. Yang 2021), though there have been many cases worldwide of intended parents changing their minds, much more prevalent than abandonment by a birth mother. It is a financial transaction in which intended parents are only required to invest money and possibly an egg and sperm, though these could also be purchased from a catalogue of donors. Whereas a child's mother used to be, by definition, she who gave birth to the child, it is now determined, including in Chinese official media, by who pays to have the child made.

Another post published by the official account of *China Women's News* on Weibo in 2019 is subtler. After stressing China's clear prohibition of surrogacy (without any legal or institutional support), it warns netizens: "The online world is not a lawless place, and you still must be responsible for your words and actions . . . No matter for what purpose, spreading rumors that surrogacy has been legalized is detestable. This problem must be managed effectively."[9]

While it is clear that surrogacy centers quietly operate in China already and advertisements for overseas surrogacy are all over the internet, the warning is meant to threaten netizens out of voicing dissent. The main actions the authorities are taking are to appease the public and suppress discussion, while tacitly allowing surrogacy.

Women Warning Women

In the women's bathrooms of many universities, hospitals, and other public spaces in China, advertisements abound for egg donors, surrogate mothers, or surrogate buyers (often providing a guarantee for a boy at a higher price). Women who are young, naive, and often short of money, such as college students, seem to be where the ideal eggs and wombs come from. However, the majority of the ads are torn up or crossed out, sometimes with warnings scrawled beside them: "Don't do it." "Your health and your body matter most." "You will earn more than that in the future." "Don't believe them." Those destroying these ads and warning their readers are a strong and growing number of ordinary women largely informed by the massive feminist presence on Weibo and how it has trickled into mainstream discussions. In the face of inaction by the authorities, women warn other women, hoping to save any women who might otherwise fall into the trap.

Awareness of the shared future of all women has always been the key point in anti-surrogacy advocacy by Weibo feminists. Some pro-surrogacy advocates view it as a class issue and argue that exploitation of the working class is inevitable and that this is no different. Also, middle and upper class women relate more easily to surrogacy buyers than to surrogate mothers. Some researchers have discussed it as "womb labor," to include commercial surrogacy in social production, said to empower and liberate women from the slavery of patriarchal families:

> Many [surrogate mothers] are negotiating with their families to gain control over their own bodies and their fertility in order to participate in this process. As surrogates, they suddenly find themselves in … a medical system that has previously been inaccessible to them as lower-class women in an anti-natalist state.
>
> Pande 2014, 5

Such an understanding coincides with the rhetoric of the one-child policy in China—a higher outside power breaks the yoke of patriarchal families on women—without seeing the underlying similarity running through that outside power and patriarchal families.

What "womb labor" produces is lives, or human beings as commodities. A Weibo feminist outspokenly called commercial surrogacy dealing in "human futures" (Juanmeng 2021a). Human babies are a commodity that can be customized with the buyers' genes—does that excuse the business of trading in human life? Weibo feminists ask why only the organs of women, womb and eggs, are marketed with the excuse of relieving the poverty of the lower class. No one mentions "poor men's freedom to make money by allowing free trade of organs"[10] (Lilylinmu 2021a).

The difference is that women's bodies have always been used as tools and commodities, while surrogacy only takes a newer, technological form. For thousands of years, patriarchal male alliances have allocated women between them. Once women enter patriarchal families, their reproduction, or their own bodies, is beyond their personal will or autonomy. In other words, using female bodies as instruments of reproduction is quite acceptable and normal in patriarchal morality. The hegemony of patriarchy has inflated to a degree that every male or every patriarchal unit is supposed to have (male) offspring, completely neglecting the cost of reproduction paid by women. Using ART to fertilize wives of men with no viable sperm and legalizing surrogacy to help infertile couples or gay men mistake male privileges for basic human rights. They are not against gay men raising children or adopting, but they are resolutely opposed to the business of making and selling children. The surrogacy industry relies on the cultural imperative of every man's right to have biologically related children, and they question this "right" for gay and straight men alike, insofar as it is achieved at the expense of coerced women's bodies. Weibo feminists call for an end to the social script of becoming a "patriarch":

> All of us should help end the urge to become a "patriarch." Don't keep asking what infertile people should do. Having an heir is not a birthright, and creating and raising a child means responsibility. When you can't bear children, you can't have children of your own genes, and no one owes you a kid. Society shouldn't guarantee a kid for everyone.[11]

Commercial surrogacy won't help poor women. They won't need the modern "medical system that has previously been inaccessible to them" in surrogacy centers if not forced by patriarchy and poverty to produce babies. This only exhibits more explicitly that the foundation of surrogacy is the enslaving of women, kept in the commodity state between patriarchal families and surrogacy centers that offer a better slavery. Furthermore, as long as the trade exists, the low-end market will always be there, and the most exploited wombs will bear the cheapest children, either for traditional patriarchal families or for the surrogate buyers. As a Weibo feminist remarked, it's not to erode the foundation of patriarchy but to expand it in transformation.

Middle class and wealthy women are also vulnerable in a society with legalized commercial surrogacy. Once reproduction can be bought in either the marriage or surrogate market, every womb is marked with a price: "The most expensive wine comes from grapes of certain vines, with every single fruit selected by hand and the temperature closely maintained during fermentation. But in the cup, it is all wine," commented a feminist on Weibo.[12] Some women wish to transfer reproductive labor to lower-class women through buying surrogacy. This also provides an illusion that women can become "male" or fathers through their economic superiority, securing offspring without pregnancy and labor. However, the potential risk and health damage in egg retrieval cannot compare with sperm donation. Upper class wives must go through the painful process to provide children as heirs of their husbands. The only difference between the privileged female buyers and the low-class "egg girl" is that the former paid money to retrieve her eggs.

In the context of patriarchal control, free will does not exist with regard to renting out one's womb. Weibo feminists oppose not only commercial surrogacy but surrogacy in all forms. In female-oriented apps such as Xiaohongshu, Meiyou, or TikTok, many pregnant women sincerely pray for the good fortune to bear sons (Xianzi 2021). A considerable portion of them will seek abortions of female fetuses, autonomously and "voluntarily."

Similarly, in a culture where having offspring is a basic right for every man, some women consider surrogacy as a little favor they could do for their male relatives or friends, as with the young Chinese woman pregnant with her future little brother for her parents. Criticism of the liberal rhetoric of choice and opportunity is key to the anti-surrogacy campaign on Weibo.

Figure 3.1 Female bodies hanging on the tree represent surrogate mothers. The dealer suggests a price to potential surrogacy customers. He is masked, suggesting how he presents surrogacy is a farce or cover-up and not the reality of it. With only money and their own needs in mind, dealer and customers ignore the shriveled body and tortured emotions caused by the exploitation of surrogate mothers. ©铁齿铜牙麻小生. All right reserved.

Reconsidering the LGBTQ Alliance

Weibo feminists pay close attention to policy changes about surrogacy in foreign countries. In addition to most European countries holding the principle that the woman who carries and gives birth to the child is the legal mother, Thailand banned commercial surrogacy in 2015 and India in 2018. New York State, however, legalized it in 2020, joining California and many other U.S. states. Weibo feminists were highly critical of this shift.

On the official webpage of New York State, it is claimed that "legalization of gestational surrogacy would allow same-sex couples and couples struggling with infertility to conceive a child through assisted reproduction."[13] This is an open declaration that anyone without a functioning womb should be righteously granted access to others' organs, on the only condition that they have the financial means to pay the fertility industry (since most of the money does not go to the surrogate mother). One Weibo feminist commented: "There are LGBTQ-supporting celebrities whose speech is broadcast on the government webpage prior to public opinion polls. It is blatant brainwashing, a campaign for the consumption of human beings. . . . What does their proclaimed respect and empathy bring to women and children?"[14] (Guozili 2020) Again, they are not opposing the LGBTQ movement, but rather the pretext of gay rights to support a massive industry built on women's exploitation. They question that having biological children of one's own is a human right for anyway, gay or straight, and argue that it is rooted in exploitative patriarchal norms.

Weibo feminists are aware that China's government is not unique in fabricating and disseminating opinions. The U.S. government's frequent indictment of China only serves to mask its own strategies of manipulation; U.S. citizens can happily imbibe manufactured options, congratulating themselves on how much more free they are than the

Chinese. In fact, lobbies and interest groups in Washington yield a bribery-like power over law-making; and a major campaign funder is the pharmaceutical industry, which has everything to gain from surrogacy.

In China, most autonomous feminists on Weibo stand steadfastly by the benefits of women and children, not afraid to launch criticism against misogynistic proposals from a male-dominated LGBTQ movement. Just as women in the 1970s in the U.S. became critical of male leadership in other social movements and founded their own feminist movement, Weibo feminists are critical of men's interests taking the lead in the LGBTQ movement. They urge women to work together, lesbian and straight, rather than sacrificing women's interests to other loyalties. This is a confusing issue, as it involves taking a stance that seems opposed to social progress; Weibo feminists consider some forms of "progress" as a regression for women. For example, in 2018, the People's Congress called for public suggestions on the modification of the Civil Law, and LGBTQ groups decided to take the opportunity to promote the legalization of homosexual marriage. A male homosexual netizen Sun Wenlin (2018) made a very detailed table of proposals, appealing to all LGBTQ supporters and feminists to join the online petition by forwarding his proposals to People's Congress website. Many feminists participated in the petition until they found a term in the table that would lead to the legalization of egg donation and surrogacy. Feminists furiously withdrew their support: "You conspire over the uteruses of my sisters, and hope that we strive for your rights?"[15] Guozili (2018), one of the most influential feminists on Weibo at that time, angrily remarked.

This incident marked the end of collaboration between gay males and feminists. In the following years, feminists have continued to criticize the surrogacy industry, which intends to find potential surrogate mothers among ordinary women and even lesbians. For example, the largest dating app for homosexual men in China, the

Blued, has included a Bluedbaby platform to introduce its users to surrogacy centers outside China, earning money as an intermediary, while a dating app for lesbians, LESDO, was purchased by an assisted reproduction technology company (Tanyancha 2019, 2020). Another lesbian app, Rela (热拉), asks users questions including: "Do you plan to form a sham (straight) marriage (*xing hun*)?" and "Are you interested in surrogacy?" (Makusishuo 2021).

Sham marriage, *xinghun*, often requires women to give birth to children using gay men's sperm through in-vitro fertilization or natural sex. Just as many lesbians and unmarried women who want to get pregnant, a single mother on Weibo, Meow's Mom, considered forming a sham marriage with a gay man, as her family could not accept her having a child out of wedlock. After joining the sham marriage "posting bar" online, she was surprised to find that literally all the gay men required women to deliver children with their sperm, and 95 percent required women to get pregnant naturally, as they could not afford in-vitro fertilization. She gave up the sham marriage plan (Meow 2021a).

In addition to sham marriage, there's also "cheat marriage," *pianhun*, meaning gay males trick women into marriage by pretending to be straight; those women are called *tongqi* (同妻) and often suffer from their husbands' cold shoulder and emotional abuse after childbirth without knowing the reason: "At least 14 million straight women in China are currently, or have been, trapped in false marriages with men who are gay," said Zhang Beichuan, a pioneer researcher on LGBT issues (Song 2016).

In 2013, Luo, a teacher and PhD candidate at Sichuan University, committed suicide after her newlywed husband acknowledged on Weibo that he was gay and had cheated her into marriage. She had spent most of her savings on him, suffered emotional abuse, and sought a divorce that he refused. The case only exposes one corner of the bitter lives of *tongqi*. Though the lives of gay men in China are certainly difficult compared with those of straight men, they have, as a whole, devised various strategies to close this gap and maintain male privilege. Weibo feminists argue that gay Chinese men have many more rights not only than lesbians but compared to all Chinese women.

Zhang Beichuan attributed the reason for cheat marriage to the social intolerance of homosexuality, and stated that gay males will not need to cheat women into marriage with the progress in social ideas. However, gay Chinese men do not necessarily want to be out of the closet, as the conservative social norms still benefit them as men. This is suggested by the situation in Taiwan. After homosexual marriage was made legal in Taiwan in 2015, 80 percent of married homosexual couples were lesbians while only 20 percent were gay male couples (*Liberty Times*, 2016). Subject to the same conservative intolerance towards homosexual groups, lesbians are eager to marry with their homosexual partners, while gay males continue to hold homosexual lovers and marry women for offspring.

In the shared patriarchal cultural context of mainland China and Taiwan, every man is supposed to have offspring of his own. He doesn't consider it immoral to utilize women's bodies for reproduction, as straight men are doing the same. Gay men fight for the same millennial male privilege as straight men to use women for reproduction, housework, and care work. Weibo feminists are opposed to this for all men, gay or straight. Granting this right to gay men further legitimates and extends the male-privilege system. In traditional Chinese culture, a man developing an intimate emotional bond with a woman was considered not only unnecessary but also shameful. As a marriage is not supposed to be built on such bonds, cheat marriages fit in fine with the norms, and being homosexual doesn't require men to give up male privilege. Although they expect feminists and lesbians to side with their causes, which many do, this is never reciprocated.

Weibo feminists point out that socially marginal yet male-dominated groups, including LGBTQ, cease to subvert patriarchy after they are promised a position within its existing mechanism and the option of exploiting women: When the revolutionary waves hit the embankment of patriarchy and find it too solid to shake ... people turn their eyes back to women. Care for children and the elderly, housework, and birth are done with the flesh and blood and emotional and mental resources of women as mothers. With the close physical and mental control of women, the reproducers of human beings, the hegemony of patriarchy can perpetuate itself forever. Women are "the prisoners who will never be released"[16] (Chuan 2021c).

Only the empowerment of women would cause patriarchal families to collapse. Weibo feminists have proposed "womb morality" to encourage women's agency in reproduction, which initiated another argument online.

The Rise of Womb Morality

The concept of womb morality reverses patriarchal moral judgements placed on women by stating the sexual and reproductive freedom are true morality. This includes women having children if they want to, regardless of marital status. If a woman does choose to marry, womb morality affirms the rightness of her giving children her surname. Womb morality includes women selecting men whose qualities seem desirable for the offspring women want, without any relationship or commitment to these men. At first glance, this might appear incompatible with Weibo feminists' anti-surrogacy stance. Surrogacy also involves choosing genetic material (egg and sperm donors) based on desirable characteristics, and many surrogacy opponents criticize this as eugenics. However, based on the biological fact that the whole process of reproduction happens in female bodies, Weibo feminists don't consider women selecting sperm from sperm banks as exploiting men in the way that surrogacy exploits disadvantaged women's bodies for corporate profit. Womb morality focuses on women using their own bodies in their own interests. It does not, however, consider "choices" such as prostitution or surrogacy as in women's own interests, no matter how needed the coercion of money might be. Legitimizing a woman's choice to rent or sell her body would excuse the deeper structural issues that would make such a "choice" necessary, according to the most followed Weibo feminist voices.

The term "womb morality" has been in use among radical feminists on Weibo for a long time. Though it's unclear who coined it originally, it fits with the daily expressions of Lin Maomao and other anti-marriage feminist bloggers. Lin suggests that mothers picking sperm of tall, handsome, and smart males to rear beautiful children is a true representation of maternal love and a social responsibility women hold for human beings. Lin's somewhat satirical suggestions have been embraced by many Weibo feminists. Women as gatekeepers to social progress through mate selection is reminiscent of early twentieth-century U.S. feminists such as Charlotte Perkins Gilman. Weibo feminists, however, use this idea to defend single motherhood. They suggest that single mothers can more consciously select genetic material without constraints such as compatibility or family stipulations. There are two facets of "womb morality": women's sexual liberty and reproductive autonomy (which are exactly what most Chinese women have been deprived of by marriage), and the more controversial aspect of social responsibility.

Attributing selecting good sperm to women's social responsibility rebukes the kidnapping of women by male-defined morality. Conservative morality judges a woman as corrupting society if she refuses to be an abstinent daughter, faithful wife, or sacrificing mother. Today, Weibo feminists declare that grasping sexual and reproductive autonomy is the most responsible behavior for the future of their nation and humanity. Strategically, they seek to adequate women's rights and women's responsibilities.

Womb morality is an empowering term embraced by many Weibo feminists including Meow's Mom, a single mother and documentary filmmaker. As a woman who received higher education outside China and planned to be a single mother for years before giving birth to her daughter, she has filmed her experiences of pregnancy, birth, and child-raising as a single mother in China. Being a single mother pits her against the bureaucracy. Deprived of healthcare and maternity leave, many single mothers are also fined when registering the birth.

Such penalties are the tip of the iceberg, as social malice against single mothers and their children is immeasurable. Comments on her videos ask where the father is and include slut-shaming and other insults. But Meow's Mom still bravely uploads her videos. Talking about raising her daughter, she said the most important thing is establishing that being a single mother is a cool thing and teaching her daughter to be proud of her family background (Meow 2021b). In a cultural context where the simple question, "Where is the father?" could bring extreme shame, womb morality equips single mothers with a shield against such violation through asserting that rearing children outside marriage conforms to natural laws and benefits society.

Because the term is a shield against a patriarchal culture that humiliates women and children, it is considered extremely offensive by the followers of patriarchy. Being single mothers in traditional Chinese society means huddling with their children in the shadows, despised and bullied. This is the punishment patriarchy lays on the natural mothers creating no father/patriarch through their reproduction. However, today a single mother can share her experiences with the public, justifying her choice and challenging the patriarchal norms through womb morality.

The most recent attack on womb morality in 2021 was initiated by several female public intellectuals. Their criticisms of womb morality include that it is a discrimination against lower-class males and that it is eugenics. Just as they previously labeled Weibo feminists "extreme feminists," they have now gone so far as to use the term "Nazis." As one Weibo feminist observed:

> If stating that not bearing children through the sperm of ugly men can be defined as Nazi, then what are those who built concentration camps and gas chambers, experimenting on human bodies and initiating genocide? . . . Losing their minds, they are only wondering how to mark those they dislike with extremist and most horrible labels to attack them . . . while talking about empathy, understanding, and tolerance when it comes to men.[17]

Weibo feminists responded with further developments of womb morality's nature and importance, contradicting the arguments of the few intellectual elites. Contrary to the accusation of eugenics, womb morality's assessment of "good sperm" does not meet one established standard, and the choice is all about the benefits and proclivities of individual women. The accusation is revealing. Claiming that poor men will be neglected is similar to rhetoric of the male-supremacist INCEL movement in the U.S., in which hostile men blame feminism for their "right" to sex with women being denied. The claim that the term discriminates against low-class males betrays the stance of those who made it, that is, the "reproduction rights" of low-class males comes before the autonomy of all women. That every man has offspring is not a human right, but a male privilege under patriarchy. Men violate women's bodies to claim that privilege every day. For example, in 2021, a 22-year-old mentally handicapped woman was married to a 55-year-old man. Although the video of the woman bursting into tears on the wedding day drew much public attention, the local authorities acquiesced to the marriage "by local custom," without a marriage certificate. Days later, the man declared that he and the woman already "slept in the same bed" (*Ifeng Weekly* 2021). Another rape happened under public eyes. A Weibo feminist mocked the liberal intellectuals as "guests beating the celebratory drums at the wedding" (Juanmeng 2021b). Meanwhile, criticism of womb morality implies that women refuse to rear children for poor men only to worship rich men and ignores that it highlights options of not rearing children or rearing children as single mothers.

An anti-marriage feminist has suggested the reason some women find womb morality irritating is precisely that they already lost sexual and reproduction autonomy. As womb morality contains "morality" and most married women cannot access the autonomy and liberation of womb morality, it implies an accusation that they are not "moral." She contests that if married women are free, why have they no right to choose not to bear children, or to use sperm other than their husbands' for reproduction, give birth to daughters only, or grant children their own surnames? (Lilylinmu 2021b).

Exposing the loss of autonomy of married women is not to criticize them but to expose the men benefitting from it. In order to spare married women implied immorality, there are feminists proposing "womb rights/power" to replace "womb morality." The few male feminists emphasize the impact womb morality exerts on existing discourse: "It's no use talking about specific matters within the existing discourse. A new term must be invented to make the majority realize there is a problem" (Zhou 2021). A feminist wrote on Douban: "If womb morality is changed to womb rights, it will be easier to be given up, losing its force, because [for women] now striving for rights is difficult while giving up tends to be praised." Another male feminist praised the term that it "like a stab, precise and fatal [to patriarchal discourse]" (L. Wang 2021).

With the emergence of womb morality and the rise of anti-marriage feminists and single mothers, patriarchy's deprivation of women's bodily autonomy represented by the only-child policy has received nuanced discussion online, rather than only criticizing the policy. Reproductive autonomy is a core topic for Chinese feminism.

It centers on individual acts of refusing marriage and Confucian filial doctrines. The discussions also give rise to the intersectional rethinking of nationalism, socialism, and Western liberalism, as will be discussed in the next chapter.

Works Cited

Babiarz, K. S., Ma, P., Song, S., and Miller, G. (2019). Population sex imbalance in China before the One-Child Policy. *Demographic Research*, 40, 319–358.

Baiheihei. (2019, February 12). 代孕这事，女人如果还意识不到 [For Surrogacy, Women Need to Realize]. Weibo. https://m.weibo. cn/1370505990/4338861288879933.

Chenzhezhe [@陈折折]. (2021, January 18). *15 年的检日, 17 年的人日都 试水过开放代孕的风口* [Procuratorate Daily in 2015 and People's Daily in 2017 Both Tested Water for Legalizing Surrogacy]. https://m.weibo. cn/1851888853/4594863243531643.

China Women's News. (2019, December 27). 炮制 *"代孕合法化" 的谣 言，当治* [Forging the Rumor of "Surrogacy Has Been Legalized" Will Receive Punishment]. Weibo. https://m.weibo. cn/2606218210/4454211405905960.

Chuan [@川 A1234567]. (2021a, January 19). *看，"后院猫"* [Look, "Backyard Cats"]. Weibo. https://m.weibo.cn/status/4595016817187167?.

Chuan [@川 A1234567]. (2021b, January 19). *前几天那个代孕退货，然后 孩子没法上户口的新闻* [On the News about the Refund of Commercial Surrogacy Leading to the Child Unable to Gain Cityzenship]. Weibo. https://m.weibo.cn/7513210373/4595207083153754

Chuan [@川 A1234567]. (2021c, March 16). *前几天，看到戴锦华老师的 一个视频被截取了一段话* [Days Before, I Saw Screenscripts from a Video of Dai Jinhua with Her Words]. Weibo. https://m.weibo. cn/7513210373/4615418783990620

Geng, X. (2017, February 9). *继续严打代孕违法违规行为* [Continue To Harshly Forbid Surrogacy That Is Against Law and Regulations]. p. A03.

Guozili [@果子狸 7777]. (2018, September 12). *我为你们发声？！我为你们挖坟！* [Voice for You?! I'd Rather Dig Your Grave!]. Weibo. https://m.weibo.cn/status/4283371259723775.

Guozili [@果子狸 7777]. (2020, April 10). *纽约州强推代孕合法，一场准备已久的绞刑* [New York State Legalized Commercial Surrogacy, a Prepared Hanging of Women]. Weibo. https://m.weibo.cn/6593893685/4492212119258665.

Heiye [@黑夜与深海]. (2021, February 4). *前阵子微博热点反对代孕掀起热烈的讨论* [Previously Heated Debates over Surrogacy Were Seen on Weibo Hot Topics]. Weibo. https://m.weibo.cn/6500973046/4600855850136176.

Hong Fincher, L. (2014). *Leftover Women: The Resurgence of Gender Inequality in China.* London & New York: Zed Books.

Huoxu [@或许不如不见]. (2021, February 11). *继承权这个事情，凭什么女孩子不能提* [Why Can't Daughters Put Forward the Issue of Inheritance]. Weibo. https://m.weibo.cn/3524285233/4603249493279017.

Ifeng Weekly [@凤凰周刊]. (2021, March 2). *民政部门调查 55 岁男子娶年轻智障女子* [The Authorities Look into the Case that 55-year-old Man Marry Young Mentally Handicapped Woman]. Weibo. https://m.weibo.cn/1267454277/4610246552586738.

Jin, H. (2015, August 7). *建国以来中国生育政策的演进* [The Evolution of Reproductive Policies since the Establishment of the People's Republic of China]. Chinagate. http://cn.chinagate.cn/news/2015-08/07/content_36248175.htm.

Juanmeng [@倦梦西洲的奋斗风]. (2021a, January 18). *人口期货* [Human Futures]. Weibo. https://m.weibo.cn/7160345268/4594827599292737.

Juanmeng [@倦梦西洲的奋斗风]. (2021b, March 3). *据说子宫道德干涉生育自由* [It Is Said that Womb Morality Hinders Reproduction Right]. Weibo. https://m.weibo.cn/status/4610580403192275?.

Jujiuwu [@居酒屋的宋枣糕]. (2020, December 7). *世界上最贵的火腿* [The Most Expensive Hams in the Word]. Weibo. https://m.weibo.cn/2606218210/4454211405905960

King, Michelle (2014). *Between Birth and Death: Female Infanticide in Nineteenth-Century China.* Stanford UP.

Li, H. (2017). 性别不公：今日乡村社会观察的一个新视角 [Social Injustice: A New Perspective to Observe the Present Chinese Rural Society]. *Wuhan University Journal (Arts & Humanity)*, 70(4), 56–60.

Li, L. (2021, January 27). 代孕遭"退单"，生物学父母有义务协助落户 [The Deserted Child in Commercial Surrogacy: Biological Parents Are Obliged to Aid the Registration]. *China Women's News*, p. 006.

Liberty Times. (2016, October 23). 6 都同志伴侶註記1280對 男女比例懸殊高達4倍 [In 1280 Homosexual Couples Registered in Six Capitals, the Number of Lesbian Couples Surpass Gays By 4 Times]. Liberty Times. https://news.ltn.com.tw/news/life/breakingnews/1864234

Lilian [@莉莉安说道]. (2021, February 28). "子宫道德"听起来刺耳是因为 [Womb Morality Is Irritating Because]. Weibo. https://m.weibo.cn/7399215761/4609550940901059

Lilylinmu [@Lily林mu]. (2021a, January 18). 反对代孕 [Anti-Surrogacy]. Weibo. m.weibo.cn/7484401377/4594751460344176.

Lilylinmu [@Lily林mu]. (2021b, March 1). 这两天为啥"子宫道德"惹众怒？因为她们没法道德 [Why Womb Morality Is Irritating? Because They Have No Womb Morality]. Weibo. https://m.weibo.cn/7484401377/4609901060686701

Makusishuo [@马库思说]. (2021, February 4). 姐姐，有个叫热拉的软件，是女同性恋交友软件 [Sister, There's an APP Named Rela, Which Is for Lesbians]. Weibo. https://m.weibo.cn/status/4600911307218616

Meow [@喵小花 Meow 她妈]. (2021a, March 20). 未婚先孕，找 gay 假结婚 [Pregnant Unmarried and Sham Marriage with Gay]. Weibo. https://m.weibo.cn/6906810540/4616952780167655

Meow [@喵小花Meow她妈]. (2021b, March 19). 未婚生孩子真的有那么难吗 [Is Being a Single Mother Really So Hard]. Weibo. https://m.weibo.cn/6906810540/4616537317315489.

Mew [@Mew_.]. (2018, November 25). 边缘人的痛苦源自什么 [What's the Origin of Pain of the Maginal Groups]. Weibo. https://m.weibo.cn/status/4310178033364501?.

National Bureau of Statistics. (2020). 人口抽样调查–按年龄分性别比 [Population Sampling Survey: Sex-ratio by Age Groups]. https://data.stats.gov.cn/easyquery.htm?cn=C01&zb=A030604&sj=2020.

Pande, A. (2014). *Wombs in Labor: Transnational Commercial Surrogacy in India*. New York: Columbia University Press.

Shi, X. (2015, December 29). 计生法修正案为什么删除 "禁止代孕" [Why the Prohibition of Surrogacy Is Deleted from the Population and Family Planning Law]. Ifeng. http://inews.ifeng.com/mip/46880773/news.shtml.

Sobotka, T. & Zhang, C. (2019). The Unexpected Rapid Normalization of the Sex Ratios at Birth in China. *2019 Annual Meeting of Population Association of America*. Austin: Population Association of America. http://paa2019.populationassociation.org/abstracts/192127

Song, J. (2016, April 22). Wives in sham marriages hidden in the shadows. *China Daily*. www.chinadaily.com.cn/opinion/2016-04/22/content_24759830.htm

Souhu News. (2021, March 11). 迟到四年的生育金：上海非婚妈妈们的抗争 [Childbirth Insurance Delayed for Four Years: The Single Mothers' Struggling in Shanghai]. Weibo. https://m.weibo.cn/status/4613655688383337?.

Sun, W. (2018, September 11). 民法典同性婚姻立法修改意见操作指南 [The Guidance for Proposes on Homosexual Marriage in the Modification of the Civil Law]. Weixin. https://mp.weixin.qq.com/s?__biz=MzI0MTE3OTk2OQ==&mid=2653301734&idx=1&sn=ac50eb9923d6e189319b6eb592773a9d.

Tianyancha [@天眼查]. (2019, September 2). *Blued* 计划赴美上市 [Blued Plans to Enter the Share Market in the US]. Weibo. https://m.weibo.cn/status/4412087214191008?.

Tianyancha [@天眼查]. (2020, January 19). 代孕产业再被曝光，关联公司股价却大涨 [While Surrogacy Service Is Exposed, the Share Price of the Related Company Is Rising Dramatically]. Weibo. https://m.weibo.cn/status/4595160212842829.

Wang, C. (2015, 12 24). 代孕问题不宜随修法 "搭车" 解决 [The Issue of Surrogacy Is Not Suitable To Be Settled Incidentally with the Change of Law]. *China Women's News*, p. A01.

Wang, J. (2017, February 3). 生不出二孩真烦恼 [It Bothers People Not Being Able to Rear the Second Child]. *The People's Daily*, p. 019.

Wang, L. (2021, March 4). 以下是在豆瓣鹅组里看到的评论 [Here Are Some Comments Found from Douban]. Weibo. https://m.weibo. cn/2602485724/4610844706472647.

Wang, Q. (2018). From "Non-governmental Organizing" to "Outer-system"— Feminism and Feminist Resistance in Post-2000 China. *Nora—Nordic Journal of Feminist and Gender Research*, 26(4), 260–277.

Xunxunzi [@-寻-寻-子-]. (2021, January 17). 之前一直以为我国女性是有完整的堕胎权的 [Before, I Thought Chinese Women Enjoyed Complete Abortion Right]. Weibo. https://m.weibo.cn/status/4594432949881750?.

Yang, Y., and Yang, H. (2021, 1 21). 郑爽的"大瓜"并不是"娱闻" [Zhengshuang's Scandal Is Not Only an Entertainment]. *China Women's News*, 004.

Yangguang [@阳光阳光闪闪亮]. (2021, February 10). 计划生育 [Childbirth Plan]. Weibo. https://m.weibo.cn/status/4603005275481853?.

Yili [@伊丽莎白骨精啊]. (2021, February 28). 一大早上就给我震撼到了 [I Was Shocked This Morning]. Weibo. https://m.weibo.cn/status/4609493851179506?.

Yingmianmian [@硬晚晚]. (2021a, February 26). 其实我对首页一些人开始自嘲"纳粹"这件事感到特别哭笑不得 [I Don't Know How to React to Some Feminists Reacting to the Accusation by Embracing the Name of Nazis]. Weibo. https://m.weibo.cn/6512113818/4608862244572038.

Zhang, H. (2021, February 26). 商业代孕入刑：保障生命尊严杜绝生育权滥用 [Adding Commercial Surrogcy into the Penal Code: Guarantee the Dignity of Life and Prohibit the Misuse of Reproductive Right]. *China Women's News*, p. 006.

Zhang, P. (2021, January 20). Chinese actress Zheng Shuang's surrogacy scandal rocks social media, prompting fresh debate over China's ban of the practice. *South China Morning Post*. www.scmp.com/news/people-culture/china-personalities/article/3118364/chinese-actress-zheng-shuangs-surrogacy

Zhao, C., and Fan, L. (2020). 论婚姻与生育的社会属性——少子化背景下浙北乡村婚育模式嬗变的田野观察 [On the Reproductive and Sociological Meaning of Marriage: A Field Study on the Evolution of

Marriage Pattern in Northern Zhejiang Province against Low Birth Rate]. *Hebei Academic Journal*, 40 (4), 198–205.

Zhou, X. (2021, Feburary 28). *如果你还是觉得"子宫道德"这个说法有攻击性* [If You Still Feel Womb Morality Aggressive]. Weibo. https://m. weibo.cn/2501511785/4609550131658953.

4

Intersectionality Under the Radar

Wuren is a combat sport trainer, lesbian novelist, psychologist, and feminist history blogger on Weibo. She also runs a unique business which she defines as intimate violence interference, that is, to help women threatened by their male partners when they seek to get out of a relationship or marriage. After realizing she was a lesbian, she divorced her husband and, when he continued to harass her and her female partner, used her combat skills to beat him up. She explains how the physical strength of men over women has been overestimated in Chinese culture. In addition to advocating for women to build their strength, she challenges the weakness mentality that has bound women psychologically. Daring to fight back makes women safer (Wuren 2021).

Like Wuren, many Weibo feminists have intersectional identities online. Based on the users' knowledge realms and the kinds of content they mainly produce, they can be identified as different kinds of bloggers by the platform, for potential audiences to find them efficiently. However, Weibo doesn't allow its users to be identified as "feminists," probably because the term is too politically sensitive. So feminists are randomly identified as intimate relations consulting bloggers (even though they are only working on reminding women of the romantic traps), showbiz news bloggers (criticizing the misogynistic misleading showbiz), and child-rearing bloggers (mothers or single mothers sharing their experience in how to raise children in a feminist way). What the bloggers actual publicize is quite opposite to the mainstream contents of the respective categories. Feminists subvert mainstream separation of their respective realms, disintegrating patriarchal constructions from different directions. This intersectionality makes it impossible for the authorities to censor and prohibit them all.

Many young women refuse marriage, and their accounts suffer repeated blocks to crack down on their popularity; they are also harassed in real life. One was slandered as a rich housewife of a prince from Saudi Arabia or a U.S. diplomat. Another young female lawyer was slandered as wife of a high-ranking official. Wrongly portraying feminists as idle, dependent, or supported by "foreign enemies," the rumors' underlying suggestion is that they are so powerful that they must belong to the most prestigious status for women under patriarchy. Shaoxi was among the first to speak out in the 2018 Chinese Me Too movement about being sexually assaulted by the vice-principal of her university. MeToo has been heavily censored in China, and feminists have resorted to creative tactics to get around this, using Chinese homophones for the sounds "MeToo": "Rice Bunny," (米兔) with emoticons of a bowl of rice and a rabbit. Though the term is unmentionable, women keep speaking up online today.

Feiyan is a married feminist with a daughter, though she holds an anti-marriage stance since awakening as a feminist. Her indomitable will to love and educate her daughter against overwhelming patriarchal odds and the affectionate stories she's shared have drawn many followers to her account. Qin Liwen, in her late 40s, has been a renowned journalist, media executive, and writer. She gradually mingled with grassroots extremist feminists on Weibo, turning from a "semi-hidden feminist" to a "women-centered feminist" (Ruobing 2021). RugglesDaCat is a former Muslim woman from the Hui minority group, while many others are PhD candidates in China and abroad.

The life experiences of these women and many others become powerful feminist narratives. With diverse education levels and backgrounds, these women form an inclusive online community. The intersectionality of Weibo feminism subverts political censorship. This chapter explores intersectional feminist expression on Weibo in four parts: the indigenization of transnational theories with criticism of Western liberalism, collaboration across national borders, feminist voices from Chinese indigenous minorities, and the restructuring of nationalism and socialism.

Indiginizing Feminist Writings

The Weibo feminist reading list includes 100 books on sociology, history, media studies, sexuality, psychology, literature, international relations and policies, economics, law, ecology, and also children's books (Claudiel 2021).

With high transnationality, intersectionality, and diversity in ideological and political camps, it includes researchers within and outside China's Party-state institutions, across countries and disciplines, from academic papers to popular readings, some of which are Chinese translations of works not yet translated into English.

For example, *Gender and Public Policy* (社会性别和公共政策) (2002) is by Li Huiying (李惠英), a feminist and communist scholar who promoted adding Gender Studies to the curriculum of the school where high officials are trained (Nan 2015). This is alongside Hannah Arendt's *The Origins of Totalitarianism* (1951) and *Women's History of the World* (1988; translation 2011) by British author Rosalind Miles. Women's literature includes a Chinese translation of *Kim Ji-young, Born 1982* by South Korean female writer Nam-joo Cho, which earned first place in the ten most spotlighted books in 2019 on Douban, a massive digital platform for readers' scoring books from home and abroad. Taiwanese female writer Lin Yinhan's autobiographical novel *The First Love Paradise of Fang Siqi* describes sexual abuse of a teenage girl by her middle-aged male Chinese teacher and looks at how

Chinese culture facilitates her rape; this was a bestseller in mainland China.

Since the market economy reform (1978) and especially with Xi Jinping's government (2012–present), dissenting views are increasingly repressed. Nonetheless, many Weibo feminists work with state institutions. Many technical workers, professionals, or researchers in the margins of institutions anonymously share feminist views on Weibo along with college students and self-educated teens. The widespread reading, sharing, and discussing of feminist works has led to a distinctly inclusive and transnational approach.

Many big bookstores across China have begun to prominently display feminist books across disciplines, as they are in demand. Feminists suggest that this responds to a deficit of information on women's perspectives and agency. It is also likely due to the massive presence of feminists on Weibo in a wide variety of disciplines and guises. The censors' strategy of forbidding feminism as a category has actually prevented its ghettoization and forced it into the mainstream. The inclusiveness of Weibo feminism, particularly valuing the writings of women from the working class and underclass with real concern for the daily lives of Chinese women, has given it widespread appeal. Feminist books from all disciplines now occupy small but prominent and eye-catching spaces in bookstores.

Some categories of transnational feminist works are especially popular and often quoted by Weibo feminists. These include intersectionality, often with race and class, and/or are relevant to the current agenda or popular topics on Weibo. Work of women from similar cultural backgrounds, such as South Korea and Japan, are particularly popular.

Transnational and interdisciplinary views are difficult for censors to evaluate, and more radical writings can be published as translations. Many foreign feminist books are anti-capitalism and highly critical of their own countries' politics. As the Chinese government considers these countries competitors or enemies, such books circulate freely in China. But when such books clearly seek to abolish all patriarchal institutions, the censors are not sure what to do with them. For example, *Patriarchal Systems and Capitalism* (Japanese, 1990; simplified Chinese, 2000) by Japanese feminist Chizuko Ueno had some parts cut before publication in mainland China. In spite of the censors, this book exhibits the inter-constructive relation between patriarchal and capitalist ruling mechanisms and was immediately popular among the Chinese. Another book by this author, *Misogyny: the Disgust with Women in Japan* (simplified Chinese, 2015), which has no English translation, is also a bestseller in China. If she were only discussing a Japanese problem, this would be unlikely.

In addition to books, Weibo feminists use a wide variety of materials. On the surname issue, to rebuke the anti-feminist assertion that "real feminists"—that is, Western ones—are not concerned with surnames (and therefore it must not be important), a feminist blogger introduced an English paper from *Signs*, "In the Name of the Mother: Feminist Opposition to the Patronym in Nineteenth-Century France." This eloquently shows that struggles over surname have been made by Western feminists as early as two hundred years ago (Eichner 2014; Juanmeng 2020). They were also voiced by early twentieth-century American sociologist Charlotte Perkins Gilman. To address the problem of rape in Chinese culture, Liang Yu (2020) quotes an article from *The Lancet* stating that 22.7 percent of Chinese men acknowledged that they had raped someone in their lives (Jewkes et al. 2013).

The wide dissemination of feminist information on Weibo is unique in the world. Although Weibo feminists express diverse and sometimes divergent perspectives, they are overwhelmingly critical of Western liberal feminism and intent on embracing transnationalism and intersectionality while including China's ethnic minorities in the discussion.

Breaking with Sino-Western Binarism

Chinese feminism's "different path" from Western feminism is often
cited by the government-run All-China Women's Federation. The
claim reflects nationalist propaganda rather than any real resistance
to reductive and eurocentric paradigms. It is true that the dominant
Western values are not applicable to the Chinese situation. However,
intentional estrangement from Western feminism and negation of the
universal meaning of some achievements is political. Sino-Western
political and ideological binarism neglects feminism in many other
countries and the opportunity for true transnationality.

The "different path" approach defends the Party-state internationally
and justifies oppression of autonomous feminism movements in
China, said to be influenced (even brainwashed) by the West. As
discussed in Chapter 2, accepting the myth of "up-down" emancipation
of Chinese women by the Party-state means blaming women
themselves for any lingering inequality. Promoting the "self-respect"
and "self-reliance" of women is the claimed agenda of the Women's
Federation. The official movement is for a "smiley Chinese feminism"
(Huang 2004) aligned with the government aim to create a
"harmonious society." Chinese women are supposed to smile through
their exploitation, continuing to work outside the home on unequal
terms and do most of the unpaid work in the home.

Since the 1980s, many NGOs have been working in China on
women's issues. Supported by foreign funds such as the U.S.-based
Ford Foundation, they function outside the Women's Federation with
projects that fit the funders' neo-liberal ideology.

These two apparently opposing sides (state feminists and Western
intellectuals) are actually from similar social strata. Government
endorsement and Western funds both require privileges, including
high positions in academia or other institutions. Even their mentalities
are fundamentally similar, ignoring feminist forces emerging from

the public. Weibo feminists combine these under a common label: "the academic group" (学院派). This does not necessarily refer to professors or researchers, but rather to all people who judge feminist expression and activism from a privileged stance.

Neither the "different path" coined by the authorities nor Western liberalism opposing Party-state institutions reflects the needs and views of the majority of Chinese women or their transnational counterparts. Blueprints drawn by intellectuals (no matter where they are from) cannot construct an inclusive, lasting, and broad feminist movement. Just as definitions do not precede phenomena, a civil movement must come first. When it does, it should be seen, recoginzed, and studied rather than judged through intellectual constructs.

On Weibo, this civil feminist movement exists and includes indigenization of transnational feminism by selecting theories applied to local issues and harshly opposing Western liberalism.

Lin Maomao, one of the most influential feminists on Weibo until her accounts were blocked from all Chinese websites in early 2021, satirized the variety of anti-feminist discourse with a "women's restroom" analogy. In a country with a population of 1.4 billion, women often need to queue before women's restrooms in busy public places, while men's rooms taking up the same space are vacant:

> The objective, neutral, egalitarian group comes up and says: Women's rights should not be privileges; we give the same space for both men's and women's rooms, and that's real feminism. The misogynistic group comes up and says: Women are indeed troublemakers and annoying. The "for your own good" group comes up and says: Women better stay home, then they won't need to line up to use a restroom. The traditional group comes up and says: It's our history, so just accept it. The "you are too angry" group comes up and says: You must have been hurt by a man in a romantic relationship, or you wouldn't be so angry. The "Pacific is over there" group comes up and says: Appreciate what you have or, we'll send you to India where there's no toilet at all.

Among all the groups, Lin identifies her least favorite: "They strive for the freedom to queue before women's restrooms. They say that some women do like queuing before using the toilets, so that they can empty their thoughts, sink into meditation, and even do some tai chi or memorize vocabulary in English."[1]

For Weibo feminists, the freedom to embrace subordination is at best a personal choice that should not be inflated into an opposition to those striving for rights. This often leads them to debating against liberal intellectuals, one example concerning Zhang Guimei (张桂梅).

The nationally renowned female principal Zhang Guimei ignited public debate by openly expressing her disapproval of a former student becoming a housewife after graduation. Seeing many girls deprived of opportunities to attend high school and forced into teenage marriage in the poor, mountainous region of Lijiang (Yunnan province), she applied for government funds to build a free girls' high school in 2008. For years, she devoted her life to helping her students gain college admission. Under her leadership, the school has achieved college acceptance rates higher than 90 percent for years, ranking first among all high schools in Lijiang. Zhang's school is also unique in that it is fully need-based. Whereas other Chinese public high schools base admission on high school entrance exam scores, Zhang selects students most in need by visiting the families herself. After years of working nearly around the clock with a very basic standard of living on campus (she donated most of her income and awards), she suffered from health problems including tumors and lung fibrosis (Huo 2020).

Zhang has been criticized for her harsh methods and strict management of the school by liberal intellectuals, some of whom claim to be feminists. A female public intellectual Voiceyaya (2020 & 2021) criticizes her disapproval of her former student becoming a housewife as "lacking primary respect [for another's' choice]." She also claims the school's motto, "I was born a high mountain not a down-flowing brook"[2] eulogizes hierarchism.

Many Weibo feminists defend Zhang. Zhang's teaching methods and concern about her students are indeed formed under an unequal hierarchal reality, which is not of her making. Anti-hierarchism should be launched at the upper authorities rather than at those who struggle to help others up from the bottom. The difficulties housewives face, from poverty and isolation to less power in the family, control of resources, and autonomy are recognized by Zhang. The rhetoric that pits housewives and feminist activists against each other is part of "divide and conquer," decreasing solidarity based on shared female status. To society overall, most housewives are less a threat than feminists such as Zhang. The call for her to respect them implicitly sides with them and with a "respect" that is both cheap and safe.

Weibo feminists highlight feminism's emancipating nature for every woman, including housewives. Another criticism of Zhang is that she has been highly praised by the authorities, which for some signals official propaganda. Zhang has used her Communist Party membership and socialist discourse to justify and seek financial support for her work, without which it probably would not be possible. Political camps should not cancel feminist deeds.

For years, Zhang gathers her students from every corner of the deep mountains and urges them at graduation to "go far away and fly high. . . . Don't come back" (Shi 2020). This goes against the national strategy to reduce poverty, which would have them work within their communities, but illustrates a desperate rescue of local young women. This makes Zhang a target of hatred from another group alongside liberal intellectuals: male supremacists, who blame her for sending potential wombs away from local men.

Transnational Activism

"Dear English-speaking sisters, we are busy fighting a chain of Chinese porn accounts that post videos of men drugging and raping girls. Please report that and follow the news with the hashtag ChinaWakeUp." This message was created by a Russian feminist on twitter, calling for joint efforts to stop some Twitter accounts from publishing videos of the rapes (Zhang 2019).

Twitter is not accessible in China due to the "great firewall," or government blocking of foreign media also including Google and YouTube. After hearing what was happening on Twitter, Guozili, a Chinese feminist, replied on Weibo in Chinese: "Drugging and raping women and uploading the videos on foreign websites has always been a big problem. My sisters and I have been making it public, but we are suppressed and receive no replies. . . . Thank you! We are waking up. Hold on for us."[3]

Mutual support and transnational, collaborative feminist activism are happening across the great firewall and language barriers. To fully understand the remarkable ChinaWakeUp case, we contextualize transnational efforts by Weibo feminists in China. Chinese feminists have always shown more empathy with women from other countries than with men of their ethnicity. They pay close attention to the trafficking of girls and women as brides from Vietnam, Myanmar, and Laos for Chinese men who cannot find Chinese wives especially in border providences. The mainstream rhetoric that whitewashes this trafficking as marriage and sympathizes with the men's families when the brides run away is fiercely criticized. For years, feminists have been attacked for exposing trafficking and pressuring Chinese police to take action (Guozili 2019; Wuhou 2020). The internet brings women together for mutual aid. A young Vietnamese woman learning Chinese in Lao Cai, Vietnam uploaded videos on the Chinese Tiktok and soon received many messages from Vietnamese women trafficked to China years before, seeking her help to contact their families in Vietnam. With joint effort across national borders, the Vietnamese woman successfully put several women in contact with their families, recording this on Tiktok and Weibo (Taoguniang 2021). Such efforts placed ongoing tragedies before public eyes.

Attentive to feminist actions beyond the great firewall, Chinese feminists on Weibo are eager to communicate with transnational feminists and respond to their concerns. Weibo feminists celebrated from afar the women's strike in Mexico in March 2020: "Sisters from Mexico, well done! Don't forget to stop doing housework, too"[4] (Luosheng 2020).

South Korean feminism is popular on Weibo because of the similar Confucian culture they oppose. Weibo feminists defend South Korean's "6B" movement, which includes no dating, no sex, no marriage, no children, and mutual support among single women. It claims to be nothing extremist but just women who "don't want to play the old game with you [men]"[5] (Yingmianmian 2020).

The shocking "Nth room" case in South Korea has lit flames of anger on Weibo. A man with the screen name "Doctor," cooperating with several men, hunted preys of young women and even teenage girls online, often tricking them into sending nude photos and then using these to blackmail them unless they met him in person. He raped them on camera and put the videos online to further control the women. The violent pornography is sold via the Telegram app, where there are over one hundred confirmed victims, and the pictures and videos have been sold to at least 60,000 men. Countless other men have watched with them, few of whom tried to contact the police (Yoon 2020). Finally, two female college students who had spied on the Nth Room with male accounts for two years collected enough evidence of sexual slavery to persuade the police to investigate.

Weibo feminists observe that sexual violence against women knows no class or national boundaries among men. Canada-owned site Pornhub also profits from footage of rapes and violence against racialized categories of women and is massively popular internationally but blocked in several countries (including China). In China, it is common for men to secretly take photos in women's restrooms and video-record having sex with women then upload these to websites outside China to attract fans and make profits. Weibo feminists are appealing to the public about this problem, while the authorities are doing nothing. As we have seen, they might take action once there is enough public pressure through cyberspace. In a country where people do not have the right to assemble and petition and demonstrators risk severe punishment, the internet offers a cloud of anonymity giving power to the public.

Faced with a solid masculine coalition globally, solidarity among women across national boundaries is also being affirmed. The Nth Room case led to global outrage at the manipulation or drugging of women to make porn videos in eastern Asia, and feminists in Russia initiated the ChinaWakeUp movement on Twitter. They even wrote instructions in Russian on how to report the videos to China's Internet Crime Reporting Center (网络违法犯罪举报网站). Weibo feminists in China responded enthusiastically, pressing the authorities to take action. The result is that Twitter banned the accounts with Chinese women drugged and raped, and Chinese police closed several Chinese websites, even while stressing that they were just "ordinary pornographic websites," not extreme like the Nth Room case in South Korea (China News, 2020). Pornography is technically illegal in China, yet pornographic videos and pictures can be accessed via various online chat rooms or minor websites, as well as all kinds of soft pornography and sexually degrading advertisements that pop up on Chinese websites and computers constantly. The government censors female-oriented novels to the degree that any physical descriptions are risky, yet turns a blind eye to misogynistic violent porn circulated online. Without netizens' insistent reporting, the authorities do not do anything.

The Nth Room case exhibits collaborative global efforts among cyber-feminists. Russian feminists were angry about the crimes against Chinese women and called for English-speaking sisters' help, and all joined the ongoing struggle of Chinese feminists against sex crimes and their sale as pornography. Global concern about sexploitation in eastern Asia that led to Twitter's ban began with exposure of the Nth Room case by feminists from South Korea. Around the globe, women dismantling patriarchal constructions help one another, and their power converges even before they come to know each other.

Voices from Minority Women in China

Approximately 120 million Chinese citizens belong to minority ethnic groups including Tibetan, Mongol, Manchu, Uygur, Hmong, and fifty others. Although minorities have their own online communities, their voices rarely reach mainstream Chinese netizens, and this is especially true of women's voices. As most of the minorities have their own patriarchal norms or replicate those of Han culture, male intellectuals and religious personnel have presented their interpretations of their groups' histories, cultures, and ethnic values to mainstream culture. It is similar to how most Western countries' knowledge about China reflects its mainstream patriarchal culture.

The emergence of Weibo feminism has changed this by gathering marginalized narratives of minority women. These range from accounts of the currently matrilineal Mosuo people to historical Mongolian queens. Such discussions have provided an empathetic and supportive online community for women from minorities to narrate their stories. RugglesDaCat (2020), for example, is a former

Muslim woman from the Hui people, which is one of the ten Islamic minorities in China. Ruggles narrated her personal experience of feminist awareness and struggling to break away from Islam, and drew much mainstream concern. Many alleged that her accounts were false and that she was not really a member of the Hui people. Weibo feminists, however, defended her with posts such as this: "Those who claim to discuss the matter based on facts are celebrating every ill-intended suspicion with ecstasy. Is the fact that they really don't care? What they want is to silence those who dissent."[6]

Ruggles could have simply been deprived of her voice had there not been a supportive community on Weibo bent on believing women and validating their diverse life experiences. Ruggles' account gathers followers at a tremendous speed, the number soon to be over 10,000.

Through her posts and a long interview with *The Planet of Sea Horse*, a feminist podcasting program created by Qin Liwen, Ruggles introduced her experience growing up in the Islamic religious culture of a Hui village in northwestern China, where girls began fasting for Ramadan at nine years old, boys at twelve. Her religious disenchantment happened during her visit to Notre Dame in Paris, where looking at the vault of the church, she suddenly realized that the one she believed had been looking at her from childhood was not Allah, but herself. It was she who sustained herself during the starving days of Ramadan as a child and led her way to a top university and occupation in a prestigious international corporation.

Ruggles has emphasized the similarities between Islam and mainstream Han Chinese culture dominated by Confucianism. Both are strict and precise "patriarchal machines." While anti-feminists on Weibo mention Muslims to claim that Han Chinese women have relatively high status and therefore should not complain, feminists have coined a new word referring to mainstream Chinese men, "*ru-slim*"(儒斯林). "*Ru*" (儒) means Confucianism and "*slim*" is short for "Muslim." The term is used to mock the nationalist sense of superiority especially regarding the status of women and to point out its hypocrisy. Linguistic innovation is common among Weibo feminists both to get around censorship and to use humor to make their points clear and accessible, especially in the face of opposition.

Saxiaoge (2021) is a Chinese Mongolian earning a PhD in Mongolian shamanistic culture in Siberia. Women in Mongolian culture enjoy higher status than among Han Chinese, and she feels most connected to her Mongolian lineage. She has gained a considerable following, as have many other women from minorities or mixed heritage, in keeping with the multicultural interests of Weibo feminists.

Unlike in the mainstream, male-dominated media, Weibo feminists seek minorities' true and diverse experiences rather than constructing them as exotic others. They have also taken anti-government and pro-minority stances on many issues. In 2020, the authorities aimed to stop using Mongolian as the teaching language in minority schools of the Inner Mongolian Autonomous Region for Chinese, History, and Politics, replacing textbooks in Mongolian with Chinese ones (Davidson 2020).

Weibo feminists spoke out against the policy and voiced support for the protests of Mongolian intellectuals. While punishing the protesters and blocking their posts, the authorities conceded to promise that other subjects would always remain taught in Mongolian (*Tenggeli News* 2020).

Many feminists demonstrate integrity, courage, and awareness of intersectionality as they support minorities. Similar to feminism, minority issues in China are much feared and suppressed. By supporting minorities' rights, Weibo feminists are among the few who dare to challenge prevailing nationalist propaganda. One strategy feminists use is to coopt official nationalist discourse and reinvent nationalism and socialism, as we will now see.

Half the Nation, Yet Without Country

In the early twentieth century, women's issues were central to the rising socialist movement against the feudal, dynastic system. One example was the push to end foot-binding, with the claim that the weakening of women leads to the weakening of the country. This issue was discussed in a feminist journal *The Women's Bell* (女界钟), founded by Jin Tianhe (金天翮) in 1903, and works of He Yinzhen (何殷震) (Liu, Karl and Ko 2013, 51 & 207). However, male leaders coopted and subordinated women's issues, delaying or ignoring concerns once they won. This is remniscent of current discourse, which asserts that once the nationalist goal of reviving China is met or class exploitation stops, women can achieve full social equality.

Class and ethnic struggles are on the rise, and Weibo feminists believe women's empowerment and leadership can help, largely due to the intersectional awareness of women who refuse to be tokenized or silenced. Feminists do not seek to silence other concerns, including nationalist or communist interests; they do seek to terminate men's monopoly in defining and interpreting nationalism and socialism.

Virginia Woolf famously wrote in *3 Guineas*, "As a woman, I have no country." But for Chinese women, it would be risky to openly state this. Anti-feminist men on Weibo twist feminist statements into claims that Chinese feminists are paid by the West to weaken China. They hope the authorities will punish Weibo feminists (with some success). They constantly fabricate "evidence of foreign support," slander Weibo feminists, and even pose as feminists in their own accounts to voice anti-government sentiments. A recent incident concerns four soldiers who died in the boundary conflict with the Indian army in June 2020 (released by official media in February 2021). One post degraded the soldiers using discourse from Weibo feminism. When caught by police, the blogger turned out to be a man attempting to frame feminists (Yingmianmian 2021). He was held for several days in detention.

As approval of the authorities can be useful for enacting social change, feminists do not want men to be the only beneficiaries of this approval. They are against the patriarchy worldwide, not specifically or especially against the Chinese government. Feminists and female communists were crucial for the establishment of the nation, which is still maintained by a female majority of professionals and technical workers, as was brought to global attention during the COVID-19 pandemic. Weibo feminists strive for political power and voice for women to match their social contributions. Also, Weibo feminism is not a disciplined or uniform organization but a powerful current formed by individuals. Some individuals are pro-state, though they are feminists first.

Some feminists take advantage of nationalist discourse to avoid risks; some devotedly redefine nationalism; some employ the power of authorities to fight back against anti-feminist males; and some are pro-state and critical of Western paradigms. These various motivations all lead in the same direction: deconstruction of the official version of nationalism.

Weibo feminists find similarities between male supremacy and white supremacy. When anti-feminist men attempt to justify inequality by arguing that most modern scientific discoveries or inventions are made by men, feminists rebuke that they are also white (so that Chinese men would also have to admit, by this logic, inferiority). The unforgettable national sufferings, or *guo chi* (国耻) due to China falling into a semi-colonial and semi-feudal (半殖民地半封建) society under Western invasions starting from the Opium War (1840) to the establishment of PRC in 1949 is stressed in official propaganda to arouse indignation of Chinese people against Western countries so that they stand by the Party-state. Shaoxi, once an influential blogger until repeated blocking of her accounts, put forward a corresponding concept of *nü chi* (女耻), the unforgettable women's sufferings. Just as Chinese people suffered from Western invasion and semi-colonization, women are subjugated by men. She calls for women to rally together around this "women's sufferings" to win true, collective emancipation. Indeed, if all women took their energy away from patriarchy, it would immediately crumble.

Coopting and changing the government's own propaganda terms is risky. The authorities strictly controlled discursive power, which is why there is so much censorship. Weibo feminism is not the Women's Federation with its government backing, and will not trade obedience for safety. Instead, feminists seize the right to define history and nationalism. The authorities are mostly men, and many of them are openly male supremacists. When feminist expressions provide fault for them to find, the consequences can be severe.

In 2019, a feminist blogger compared the Nanjing Massacre by the Japanese invading army in the Second World War in 1937 and the killing of women through female infanticide and selective abortion. The Nanjing Massacre is a national trauma: Japanese soldiers killed approximately 300,000 civilians (including children) and unarmed soldiers, and they raped many women in the six weeks after seizing the then-capital city. She suggested that selective abortion and female infanticide have caused far more loss of Chinese lives than the Japanese army did. The official account of the Communist Youth League (2019) extracted some lines from the original post to frame the blogger as supporting the Japanese army.

When the blogger defended herself, the operator behind the Youth League account contacted the local police station requiring them to imprison her for "picking quarrels and provoking trouble," a famous catch-all crime to punish any misbehaviors that do not fit in a more specific category. However, the local police station refused to do so. In their eyes, the blogger had made her point quite clear and the

Communist Youth League's misinterpretation is ridiculous. Apparently, operating an official account makes some overestimate their power. This was shortly before their steering of public opinion came to a full-blown propaganda disaster when feminists took over the cartoon idol Jiang Shanjiao (discussed in Chapter 1). The authorities are not a monolithic force; they are composed of individuals who do not necessarily agree on tactics, and some are more honest than others. Not all of them want to persecute feminists, and doing so is risky in the cyber age wherein Weibo feminists have become adept at exposing injustice. When feminists use national symbols with conviction and respect, this makes it harder for the government to find fault.

Weibo feminists emphasize that women make up half the people. A nationalism that neglects or excludes women is not truly patriotic, and Weibo feminists do not launch gratuitous attacks on the nation and its symbols. The twelve netizens caught and arrested for humiliating national heroes were all men posing as feminists to slander the movement. Behind their ironically miscalculated deeds, such anti-feminist men exhibit a lack of awareness not only of feminism but also of civil politics. Their irreverent comments about national politics alert government censors as much as the feminists they hate. A high-handed authoritarian government is hostile to civil discussions of politics and can silence anyone it likes, even the ones singing the praises of the authorities.

Breaking through the maze of patriarchal culture, Weibo feminists have set a norm for artfully applying the authorities' own rhetoric while pursuing rigorous research and transparent actions that appeal to the public (such as donations to frontline workers). Prominent women on Weibo deconstruct and restructure socialism in a way that is grounded in such deep and respectful knowledge that it is difficult for the authorities to openly criticize it.

Socialist Feminism: Intersectional Discussions of Women and Class

> Let's examine why women are persecuted by men and have failed to emancipate themselves for thousands of years. . . . What weaknesses on earth are laid on women? . . . Physical vulnerability just results from customs, as bound feet don't exist until they are bound, so these are not rooted physical weaknesses. The only weakness in women, if we must find one, lies in reproduction.[7]

This excerpt is from an article by Mao Zedong (1893–1976) written in 1919 when he was 26 years old. After denying any physical inferiority of women, he asserts that women are exploited and persecuted because of their role in reproduction. He then gives his strategy for uprooting inequality: guarantee women's economic independence through education and participation in social production and establish social infrastructure assisting women with childbirth and childcare. Such initiatives were put in place with the founding of People's Republic in 1949.

Although the communist ideals have been totally discarded in current politics, the authorities can hardly censor them, and anti-feminist men cannot openly criticize them, as the early communist heroes continue to shine in state propaganda. The same is true of Engels, who was outspoken about the exploitative nature of marriage and whose quotes will not be attacked by censors, as he figures prominently in the national narrative.

Socialists on Weibo also quote early communists to protest against the current authorities. With the market economy reform (1978), previous social infrastructure such as daycare centers in workplaces gradually disappeared, worsening discrimination against women. Inspecting Team of Gender Discrimination in the Job Market (2020), a Weibo account, cites statistics on the low percentage of women in government today, with a citation from Mao Zedong. In a talk with a women's delegation from Yugoslavia in 1956, Mao considered women's political participation in China far from sufficient and said that in the communist government, female and male comrades should be at least equally represented. In the 1950s, this began to be put in practice, with greater female presence in government than in Western countries of the time (Ding 1993, 12). The post has been reposted thousands of times, expressing a dissatisfaction with the current official advocacy of traditional gender norms.

Weibo feminists consider the individual deeds of historical figures rather than the movements they were affiliated with. They are well aware that women, as T. Eagleton acknowledged, "have been dumped and discarded as often by traditional leftists as by the [current] system itself" (1996, 28). They reforge the heritage of Marxist discourse into women-centered feminist politics.

In December 2020, a 23-year-old female employee of Pin Duo Duo, one of China's largest e-commerce corporations, died on her way home from overtime work at 1:30 a.m. Exploitation in Chinese companies is known as the "996 pattern," that is, working from 9:00 a.m. to 9:00 p.m. six days a week. Many employees, such as this young woman, actually work longer than that without being paid at all for the extra hours. The load of work is so heavy that employees can't finish it unless working extra hours "voluntarily." Subsequently, a man Wangtaixu (2021) released a video on Weibo saying that he was fired by Pin Duo Duo because he witnessed his colleague being taken away by an ambulance from the office and uploaded the picture to an anonymous online forum. He also exposed that in some sections, there are implicit rules requiring employees to work 300 to 380 hours a month. Pin Duo Duo (2021) judged his exposure "extremist" and reaffirmed his discharge. In a country where the Workers' Union is a token organization led by the Party (even more marginalized in politics than the All-China Women's Federation), whose only function is to forbid workers from forming a union of their own, these employees have few choices other than to accept the heavy exploitation.

Many male bloggers voice women-hating sentiments while also protesting capitalism's over-exploitation. Wang, who produced the anti-exploitation video, was found to have joked about feminism in an interaction with a famous anti-feminist account on Weibo. Others mocked feminists' overreaction to the death of a "slut," or concluded that behind every man who dies in the "996 pattern," there is a vain and insatiable woman, ignoring the fact that the one died actually was a woman (Heimingdan 2021).

A Weibo feminist remarked: "Why do we say women's rights are the basis of human rights? ... Class oppression, which seems to have no relation to gender, can only be established on the premise that the oppression of women enables a food chain of deprivation of people starting from the deprivation of women in the substrates of everyday lives."[8] She substantiated her argument with various sources, including the historical facts that in the U.S., white women were protected from their husbands' beating by law 19 years after the emancipation of black slaves and gained the right to vote 55 years after black males. Another feminist explains it in a more explicit way: "The premise for you to do a '996 pattern' job is that you can have food, clean clothes, comfortable beds, and someone babysitting your children and taking care of your elders. ... When entering the job market, women suffer unequal pay and exploitation, taken advantage of by capitalism either way."[9]

The blogger also shared an interesting economic term describing increasing exploitation of labor: "global housewifization of labor" (Ueno 1990/2020, 252), meaning employment is getting informal, unstable, more exploited but without promotion channels, reliable insurance or lawful protection, just as the work of housewives. She ironized: "So they [the economists who coined the term] actually know that being required to work overtime when needed ... and be kicked away when not, without labor insurance, welfare, or a formal contract, is exploitation."[10] Women have been constrained to the housewife position for thousands of years, but only men who are slipping into a similar condition deserve intellectual attention. Only exploiting men is considered as exploitation, while exploiting women is just a normal situation.

One comment under the post concludes: employment under the "996 pattern" just gives men an experience of women's ordinary lives. These articles and discussions address why Marxist and socialist movements failed to resolve the exploitation of women's labor in social production and reproduction and maintained inequality between the sexes. Under patriarchy, based on half of human beings' unpaid or low-paid labor and on the limitation and usurpation of women's natural rights over offspring they bare, the ideal of a classless society is both hypocritical and impossible.

Ma Jinyu (马金瑜) is a former journalist married to a local man in a Tibetan region of Qinghai Province. She suffered serious domestic violence for years. Although she ran a business increasing the incomes of many families in the region using her knowledge and connections to the media, local men were still hostile to her and required her husband to beat her and teach her to be submissive. Hou Hongbin, a famous feminist on Weibo whose account was blocked in April 2021, compared her situation with similar obstacles to poverty alleviation around the globe in *Half the Sky: Turning Oppression into Opportunity for Women Worldwide* (English 2010; Chinese 2014), and commented:

> If you want to enrich a poor region, the first step is finding a proper program, and the second, letting women make decisions for their families. The second step is hundreds or even thousands of times harder that the first one. Women who make money for their families are still being beaten and forced to give the money they earned away to the husbands who spend it on prostitutes while kids starve.... The inequality between men and women is greater than any inequality between classes.[11]

People who still stress that class is a priority over gender today on Weibo do not care about class, inequalities, or exploitations. They intend to maintain a history and politics that are primarily about men. Socialism must intersect with feminism to become a viable system based on more than ideals.

From Intersectional Criticism to Activism

Although Weibo feminists integrate a feminist agenda into the everyday life of individuals, it doesn't mean they have given up influencing public issues. On the contrary, feminists on Weibo have responded to public issues in an autonomous, unorganized and flexible way, imposing pressure on the authorities and resisting the overwhelming misogynistic culture.

Feminist voices online serve as a means of public supervision, and pressing the authorities to act can be illustrated in the scandal of the Spring Bud Project in 2019. Initiated in 1989, the Spring Bud Project is a charity project run by China Children and Teenage Fund under the All-China Women's Federation, which has always been publicized as to aid girls only in the poor regions while raising public donations. However, in 2019, the project was found by netizens that half of its fund had been allocated to boys, including for a nineteen-year-old boy in Beijing to buy a camera.

Weibo feminists launched fierce criticism online against the project cheating public donors (many individual donors are women with the hope of helping the young versions of themselves) by misappropriation of the fund. The project uses pictures of poor girls to raise public sympathy, and then allocates funds raised to boys. More importantly, such misappropriation has been going on for years almost publicly— the allocation details listed in tables can be found online, but no one had paid any attention or bothered to question the authorities.

Resources, even declared for girls only, are so easily and naturally diverted to men, exposing a small part of the iceberg of the misogynistic mechanism hidden under water.

The feminists' blogs soon suffered harsh censors, with many accounts blocked. Some accounts publicized pictures instead of texts in order to avoid the censors. Facing harsh censoring checking texts and images online to crack down on the protesting voice, several feminists came up with a new idea. They printed the protesting pictures about the Spring Bud Project on goods such as T-shirts and phone covers and sold them on Taobao, the leading e-commerce site in China. This brought them a lot of trouble: their shop on Taobao was shut down with all deposit money paid by customers frozen, causing a total loss of tens of thousands of yuan. They are still forbidden from opening shops on Taobao today.

At the beginning of 2020, the All-China Women's Federation, the administrating institution of the project, published a notification acknowledging its misappropriation and announcing that all the funds allocated to boys had been refunded to donors and the relevant officers had been punished (*China Women's News* 2020). Despite the sacrifice made, feminists earned a positive response, which exhibits the civil right to examine government work and educates the public that women's interests matter.

Another incident concerns feminists confronting a more demotic misogynistic case. In 2020, a female student in China's top Tsinghua University accused a male student of sexual harassment in the canteen but later acknowledged that she had made a mistake after watching the monitoring video and offered an apology. Though both sides have already clarified the whole incident in the online forum of the university, it still went public on Weibo. Many anti-feminist male bloggers, taking advantage of the opportunity, launched cyberbullying attacks against the female student, exposing her personal identity, and attacked the whole Me Too movement as persecuting innocent men.

During the flaming arguments, supporters of the female students received violent cartoon pictures of a dismembered nude female body. Then, a circle producing and consuming the extremely violent and anti-women pornographic cartoons was brought into the public eyes.

Created by Jiang Minghui (蒋明辉), the JM Empire cartoon imagined an extreme patriarchal hierarchal world inspired by the Japanese military mechanism during the Second World War, where all women are used as sex slaves for all men. Cutting up newborn babies and infusing them back into the mothers' bodies and peeling off the skin of a feminist and using her as a public sex toy shocked the public. For a long time, such cartoons, technically illegal in China, have been traded freely on Taobao, so that they could reach anyone, including children.

Still, some liberal bloggers argued that it is only a non-mainstream sexual fantasy, and called for it not to be reported to the authorities so as to support freedom of creation. Jiang Minghui's team shrewdly lied to the public that they were already under police investigation, which aroused another liberal attack on feminists persecuting freedoms.

However, far from the liberal utterances that the cartoon is a mere fantasy and irrelevant to the real world, it relates to normal reality more closely than anyone could expect. First, it has already been used to threaten women, from the female student in Tsinghua University to feminists online. An anti-feminist threatened to shred feminists into nutritional powder for "my own female dog," meaning his wife or female partner, pregnant at home. Second, the settings, though extremely anti-human, are quite identical with many historical or current realities, for example, abandoning abortion and contraception, forced prostitution in the Japanese army, female infanticide, degrading women as animals, controlling women's minds with patriotism and sending them into suicide attacks, and the worship of patriarchal hierarchal order and war. As a pornographic cartoons, they revealingly seldom showed any sexual gestures but provided long texts of world settings. What aroused the audience was not sex itself but a political mechanism wherein they could persecute women and children freely.

This is not an imaginary fantasy but a collage of anti-women politics. While some Weibo feminists explain such points on their blogs, one feminist went straight to the police station in Beijing with the materials gathered online. Based on their women-centered stance, Weibo feminists refuse to be coaxed in political spectrums from left-wing socialism to liberalism; they'd like to take advantage of all possible resources to make the world a better place for women to live in. Soon, the police arrested Jiang Minghui, and the anti-pornography office led by the Publicity Department of the Communist Party of China made a public announcement especially condemning the anti-women content (Xiaoxiang Morning News 2020). The JM Empire Superchat[12] is still on Weibo.

Works Cited

China News. (2020, July 9). 全国"扫黄打非"办：快速处置所谓"国内版N号房网站" [National Anti-pornography Office: Quickly Handle the So-called Domestic Nth Room]. Weibo. https://m.weibo.cn/1784473157/4524725563225665.

China Women's News. (2020, January 10). 坚守"春蕾计划"初衷，助力"春蕾"成长成才 [Hold Fast to the Spring Bud Project, Aiding the Growth of the Spring Bud]. Weibo. https://m.weibo.cn/status/4459290645431751?.

Chuan [@川A1234567]. (2021b, January 26). 今天我对着一个经济学名词笑了整整三分钟 [I Was Laughing Over An Economic Term for Three Minutes Today]. Weibo. https://m.weibo.cn/2606218210/4454211405905960.

Chuan [@川A1234567]. (2021a, January 10). 想解决韭菜的问题，先解决韭菜他妈的问题 [To Settle the Problem of Labor, Settle the Problem of Labors' Mothers First]. Weibo. https://weibo.com/ttarticle/x/m/show/id/2309404591951109292043?_wb_client_=1.

Claudiel [@claudiel]. (2021, January 12). 女权书单更新啦[The Update of Feminist Reading List]. Weibo. https://m.weibo.cn/status/4592668862066856?.

Communist Youth League. (2019, November 4). 某大V借民族苦痛历史散布性别仇恨言论 [A Poster Spread Hatred Speech Taking Advantage of the Bitter History of the Nation]. Weibo. https://m.weibo.cn/3937348351/4435055457723501.

Davidson, H. (2020, September 1). Inner Mongolia protests at China's plans to bring in Mandarin-only lessons. *The Guardian*. www.theguardian.com/world/2020/sep/01/inner-mongolia-mandarin-schools-language-protests-china-mandarin-schools-language.

Ding, J. (1993). 毛泽东关于中国妇女解放道路的思想 [Mao Zedong's Thoughts on the Approach to Chinese Women's Emancipation]. *Journal of Chinese Women's Studies*, 04, pp. 8–12.

Eagleton, T. (1996). *The Illusion of Postmodernism*. Oxford: Blackwell Publishing.

Eichner, C. J. (2014). In the Name of the Mother: Feminist Opposition to the Patronym in Nineteenth-Century France. *Signs*, 39(3), 659–683.

Fu, X. (2013, January 7). "川大同妻自杀案"一审：死者家人诉讼被驳回[The First Instance of the Sucide Case of Tong Qi in Sichuan University: the Woman's Families' Appeal Rejected]. Sohu News. http://news.sohu.com/20130107/n362599824.shtml.

Guozili [@果子狸 7777]. (2019, March 3). 越南75%的拐卖目的地是中国[China Is the Main Destination for Vietnamese Trafficking Victims]. Weibo. https://m.weibo.cn/6593893685/4338071405780029.

Guozili [@果 子 狸 7777]. (2019, May 29). China Wake Up. Weibo. https://m.weibo.cn/6593893685/4377249560154884.

Heimingdan [@黑 名 单]. (2021, January 12). 这就是蛹人 [This Is Men]. Weibo. https://m.weibo.cn/6873443241/4592567826778523.

Huang, L. (2004). 中国女性主义 [Feminism in China]. Guangxi: Guangxi Normal University Press.

Huo, S. (2020, November 18). 靠唱红歌、苦学，她让1800多名穷女孩考上大学，张桂梅的神话能复制吗 [By Singing Red Songs and Studying Hard, She Sent 1800 Poor Girls to Universities. Can Zhang Guimei's Myth Be Copied?]. Weibo. https://weibo.com/ttarticle/x/m/show/id/2309404572650109534726?_wb_client_=1

Huoxu [@或许不如不见]. (2021, January 12). 为什么说女人的权利是最基础的权利[Why We Say Women's Right is the Baseline of Human Right]. Weibo. https://m.weibo.cn/3524285233/4592489422393740.

Inspecting Team [@就业性别歧视监察大队]. 妇女参政论 [Women's Political Publication]. Weibo. https://weibo.com/5327831786/JtdLluhxI?type=comment#_rnd1617522987560.

Jewkes, R., Fulu, E., Roselli, T., and Garcia-Moreno, C. (2013). Prevalence of and Factors Associated With Non-Partner Rape Perpetration: Findings from the UN Multi-country Cross-sectional Study on Men and Violence in Asia and the Pacific. *The Lancet Global Health*, 1(4), e208–e218.

Juanmeng [@倦梦西洲的奋斗风]. (2020, May 19). 西方女性争取冠姓权的历史 [The History of Western Feminists Striving for Surname Rigt]. Weibo. https://m.weibo.cn/status/4506084079096940?.

Liang, Y [@梁钰 stacey]. (2020, May 17). 中国有近四分之一的男性承认自己有过强奸行为 [Nearly ¼ Males in China Acknowledged That They Had Raped Someone]. Weibo. https://m.weibo.cn/status/4505683120709644 ?

Liu, L. H., Karl, R. E., and Ko, Dorothy (Ed.). (2013). *The Birth of Chinese Feminism: Essential Texts in Transnational Theory*. Columbia University Press.

Luosheng [@我是落生]. (2020, March 10). 墨西哥姐妹们，记得家务劳动罢工啊 [Sisters from Mexico, Don't Forget to Stop Doing Housework]. Weibo. https://m.weibo.cn/5822334131/4480923636398525.

Mao, Z. (2008). 女子自立问题 [The Issue of Women's Independence]. In *The Early Articles of Mao Zedong: 1912–1920*, pp. 383–385. Changsha: Hunan People's Publishing House.

Nan, C. (2015, May 26). 李惠英：为让中央党校开设社会性别课，我蛮拼的 [Li Huiying: I strove with all my energy to introduce gender class in the Party School of Central Committee]. *China Women's News*, p. B2.

Pin Duo Duo [@拼多多]. (2021, January 11). 关于员工王某多次在某匿名社区发布"极端言论"被公司解约的情况说明 [An Notification about the Former Employee Wang Publicizing Extremist Utterances and Being Discharged by the Company]. Weibo. https://m.weibo.cn/2606218210/4454211405905960.

Ruobing. (2021, January 14). 《海马星球》覃里雯：我是如何进化为"女本位"的女权主义者 [Qian Liwen with The Planet of the Sea Horse:

How I Evolve into Women-centered Feminists]. The Paper. https://m. thepaper.cn/baijiahao_10762445.

Saxiaoge [@卅肖格]. (2021, February 21). 微博对我而言逐渐失去了意义 [Weibo Loses Meaning for Me]. Weibo. https://m.weibo.cn/ status/4607168210537938?.

Shi, A. (2020, July 2). 把1600多名女孩送出大山的女校长：这才是真正 的"姐姐来了" [Female Principal Sending 1600 Girls out of the Mountain: Sisters Are Coming]. Ifeng. https://ishare.ifeng. com/c/s/7xmh0Otqa1S.

Taoguniang [@越南桃姑娘]. (2020, April 2). 越南姑娘去中国12年第一次跟 妈妈打电话[Vietnamese Girl Spoke to Her Mom for the First Time after 12 Years' Separation]. Weibo. https://m.weibo.cn/7480950994/4621635199700111.

Tenggeli News [腾格里新闻]. (2020, September 4). "五个不变"如何落 地 自治区教育厅权威回应[How to Guarantee the "Five Not to Change," the Authoritative Response from the Educational Bureau of the Autonomous Region]. Weibo. https://m.thepaper.cn/newsDetail_ forward_9042089.

Ueno, C. (1990/2020). *Patriarchal System of Capitalism.* (Y. Zou, & M. Xue, Trans.) Hang Zhou: Zhejiang University Press.

Voiceyaya. (2020, October 28). 别在那感动自我了 [Don't Indulge in Self-empathy]. Weibo. https://m.weibo.cn/1542701343/4565027090333963.

Voiceyaya. (2020, January 3). 顺 便 说 一 句 [By the Way]. Weibo. https://m.weibo.cn/status/4589199414002329?.

Wangtaixu [@王太虚 wray]. (2021, January 10). 因为看到同事被抬上救护 车我被拼多多开除了 [I Was Fired by Pin Duo Duo For Witnessing My Colleage Carried to An Ambulance]. Weibo. https://m.weibo. cn/1544481381/4591917712809183.

Wesoky, S. R. (2016). Politics at the Local-Global Intersection: Meanings of Bentuhua and Transnational feminism in China. *Asian Studies Review*, *40*(1), 53–69.

Wuhou [@午后的水妖]. (2020, March 3). 打着婚姻旗号的人口买卖 [Population Trafficking in the Name of Marrigae]. Weibo. https://m. weibo.cn/2606218210/4454211405905960.

Wuren [@写百合的无人]. (2021, February 2). 街头格斗知识科普 [Some Combat Skills Used in Actual Fighting]. Weibo. https://m.weibo. cn/5191030913/4600280488347218.

Xiaoshan [@小珊 liang3]. (2020, October 18). 一个女人开口说话的代价 [The Cost for A Woman Speaking Aloud]. Weibo. https://m.weibo. cn/7229051325/4561485772885365.

Xiaoxiang Morning News. 全国扫黄打非办：淫秽漫画作者JM被拘 留[The National Anti-pornography Office: the Author of Pornographic Cartoon Is Arrested]. Baijiahao. https://baijiahao.baidu. com/s?id=1686862429771605397&wfr=spider&for=pc.

Xie, B. H. (2021, 2 2). 街头格斗知识科普.

Yingmianmian [@硬 晚 晚]. (2020, November 2). 我 非 常 反 感 [I Dislike It]. Weibo. https://m.weibo.cn/6512113818/4566849620288140.

Yingmianmian [@硬晚晚]. (2021, February 21). 真是大水冲了龙王庙的好 戏[Such A Great Drama]. Weibo. https://m.weibo.cn/6512113818/ 4607141618651068.

Yoon, S.-Y. (2020, March 29). "Nth Room": A Digital Prison of Sexual Slavery. Korean Joongang Daily. https://koreajoongangdaily.joins. com/2020/03/29/features/DEBRIEFING-Nth-room-A-digital-prison-of-sexual-slavery/3075441.html.

Zhang, P. (2019, June 10). ChinaWakeUp a call to action as women expose Twitter accounts selling date-rape drugs, porn. *The Star*. www.thestar. com.my/tech/tech-news/2019/06/10/chinawakeup-a-call-to-action-as-women-expose-twitter-accounts-selling-daterape-drugs-porn.

5

The Politics of Feminist Word-play

Taiwanese author Lin Yihan's semi-autobiographical novel *Fang Siqi's First Love Paradise* (2017) was well-received in mainland China. This suggests that although the politics of Taiwan and mainland China are very different, the cultural patterns of violence against women described in this novel are the same. Chinese women share specific traumatic experiences across political climates and the same urgent need to break through a thousand-year tradition of male violence supported by linguistic conventions. As Lin reflected about her protagonist in an interview: "She suddenly realized that it was not those who studied literature but literature itself that betrayed her."[1] The protagonist is a twelve-year-old girl sexually abused by her fifty-year-old Chinese teacher. Lin emphasized that the novel is not about how a girl was raped but about how she fell in love with the rapist. It was "tenderness" that pushed her to total destruction.

This "love" originates from the protagonist's pious belief in Chinese literature. She let a thousand-year-old lyrical language seep into her soul. This is precisely the language of pedophiles and rapists. The enchanting mind trap to capture innocent sex prey was not constructed by this particular rapist. His identity as a Chinese teacher—his eloquence, erudition, and rhetoric—all point to millennia of linguistic conspiracy.

Just eight days after this interview, Lin Yihan committed suicide at the age of twenty-six, adding a painful endnote to her impressive message: "This type of rape is the largest massacre in the history of human beings"[2] (Lin 2017). What exactly is "this type of rape"? There is a great power disparity in it, which enables and justifies the abuse of young women's bodies. This exceeds inequalities on the individual level; it is a public disaster comparable to genocide. Rape is accomplished by the joint effort of the whole society, including (and especially) language.

During the rape, "He penetrated her body by force and she apologized for it"[3] (Lin 2018, 24), because every word she could utter turned into an apology when with this man. Embedded in her attempt to figure out the situation and protect herself was a cultural entity constructed in the realm of language. A similar linguistic oppression is described by Japanese reporter Shiori Itō (2019) when narrating her rape by Noriyuki Yamaguchi, a prominent newscaster:

> To Yamaguchi, my superior, I had always used honorifics. I could hardly say any words naturally to express protesting from an equal position that would be suitable for a woman to employ with a senior male of higher social status. Perhaps there are no such words in Japanese.
>
> 37

This alienation doesn't only happen at the word level. The novel repeatedly emphasizes the role that ancient Chinese literature plays in the rape. Literary quotations spring up in the speech of the rapist and help him lure women. The narrator remarks: "Discourse swells up in front of beautiful women just as an erect penis"[4] (Lin 2018, 35). Monique Wittig (1992) has noted that "any important literary work is like the Trojan Horse at the time it is produced. Any work with a new form operates as a war machine" (68). Here, the analogy might be reversed, with the Trojan Horse acting as the male-defined literary canon stealthily invading and then taking over women's minds. When women accept and integrate these canons, the artistry along with the subjugated status of women are built into their identity. These are difficult to conquer, as they have become part of themselves. Since its formation, the self has been buried in the seeds of its own annihilation.

Chinese women struggling for autonomy need to reconcile with their ethnic identity rather than lingering forever between the modern/Western and the traditional/national. This explains the significance of linguistic innovations by feminists on Weibo. Language is both a kind of politics in itself and the material for restoring women's ideology and artistry.

Creation of words by feminists in online arguments strike back against verbal attacks. Politically, verbal innovation rebels against the mainstream disciplinary discourse that authoritarianism has extended into language. Culturally, it is a protest against a context ridden with insulting words relating to women. It has liberated Chinese women's righteous rage, terminating the unarmed linguistic state of the past. Feminists are redefining texts and literature to reframe Chinese language and identity. They not only demand that literature recognize women but also that women rediscover and recreate literature.

Although Lin Yihan accurately depicted the links between rape, language, and mental colonization and their tremendous impact on individuals and society, she herself did not seem to overcome the colonizing effects of male literature. Weibo feminists might have asked her to forget Baudelaire, Naipaul, Tolstoy, Kenzaburo Oe, Fitzgerald, and Confucius—names mentioned by her in the interview. They might have asked her to forget these prestigious names, which have gone down in literary history and will keep shining, and turn her eyes to a darker corner and to noises made by garrulous women despised by the gilded literary traditions. Just as turning the eyes from filament lamps to the dark night sky, at first it is all black—but as the eyes get used to it, one begins to see stars. These are the self-defensive language, the booming creativity, and the sacred temples of women.

Politics in Characters

On Weibo, topics pertaining to women's rights easily trigger flaming arguments. Verbal attacks and hate speech appear more fiercely on online platforms than elsewhere. Compared to the language of a matrilineal minority such as the Mosuo people (摩梭人), standard Chinese has many more insulting words for sexual organs and behaviors, especially targeting women (Xu Ruijuan 2014, 194). This difference suggests that language functions as a tool for punishment and discipline. For example, verbal attacks on women who have lost their virginity before marriage to someone other than their future husbands have provided a scene of public execution of "sluts" online. "Black fungus" (黑木耳) is a term referring to vulvas with rich sexual experiences, and it is also used to humiliate any woman who wants to express any ideas of her own. This word has brought much anxiety to young women, who fear that the color of their vulvas is not pink enough. Reassuring, protesting, or explaining biological common sense would never succeed in eliminating the abusive force of this kind of verbal attack. But this pain finally ceased after feminists invented "needle mushroom" (金针菇), referring to the penis that fears being measured or falling short.[5]

The idiomatic retaliation of "needle mushroom" not only combats "black fungus" but also the term "easy girl" (used in English). Chinese male netizens coined "easy girl" to criticize their female compatriots who prefer foreign men. They say it is because foreigners have larger penises. This is reminiscent of the involuntary celibate or "incel" movement of male supremacy in the United States that blames women for choosing men other than themselves on superficial criteria. Their Chinese counterparts go as far as to blame the spread of HIV/AIDS in China on female college students getting infected by black sexual partners. Such accusations decreased, however, in the face of "needle mushroom." Employing insulting sex-related words used to be a male privilege. When women begin to taunt male bodies openly, they grasp a defensive power against verbal abuse. Essentially, they beat male supremacists at their own game.

Insulting, abusive, and disciplinary words targeting women do not just exist in online platforms but are also deliberately fostered by government-sponsored media. This betrays the underlying patriarchal structure of China's authoritarian regime. Leta Hong Fincher's *Leftover Women* (2014) clearly traces how the official departments and mouthpieces of China's Communist Party promoted the term "leftover women" (剩女) to stigmatize urban, educated, professional single women. Contrary to the imposed anxiety of women being left behind in the marriage market, it is actually men who struggle to find wives due to sex ratio imbalance from decades of selective abortion of female fetuses. Men outnumber women by more than 30 million in the overall population and, as women live longer, the imbalance would just be more serious among younger generations.[6] The authorities urge women to rush into marriage in their late twenties because they are worried that the men who cannot find wives will threaten "social stability," or more explicitly, the stability of the communist regime: "In one sense, leftover women do not exist. They are a category of women concocted by the government to achieve its demographic goals of promoting marriage, planning population, and maintaining social stability" (Hong Fincher 2014, 6).

The government engineered this reversal to brainwash women into marrying the "surplus men" whose bachelorhood could otherwise cause social unrest, as could, in a different way, the rise of single, independent women. Although the term crept into all strata of society—with images ridiculing single women as sad, lonely, and pathetic—and did scare some women into marriage, the strategy was not as successful as the government had hoped it would be. It was eventually modified so that rather than discouraging women from higher study and professional advancement on the grounds that this would lead to tragic spinsterhood, it told them instead they could have it all. Replacing women with graduation gowns alone and in tears, current images portray them with baby in one arm, diploma in the other. Predictably, no measures have been taken to make it easier for women to juggle professional and family life.

Weibo feminists have been instrumental in the ongoing defeat of the leftover women caricature. To resist the stigmatization of single women as "leftover" and to point out the male-benefiting nature of marriage as a patriarchal institution, feminists continue to invent new terms such as *bu hun nü* (不婚女), meaning women who choose not to get married, in place of *wei hun nü* (未婚女), or unmarried women. The difference is, "*wei*" (未) in the later term means future, so "*wei hun nü*" actually mains women to be married, while "*bu*" (不), meaning no, makes a clear manifestation of the refusal of marriage. Another term *ke hun nan* (渴婚男) means men who are eager (literally "thirst") to get married. But the most widespread term on Weibo that illustrates the exploitative nature of marital relations may be *kang da ding* (扛大鼎). *Ding*, an ancient Chinese cooking and ritual vessel usually made of bronze, refers to the husband, so that *kang da ding* literally means "carrying the heavy giant ding on the back." This term vividly describes the burden of wives' obligations, including patrilocal residence, unpaid housework, sex on demand (Chinese law doesn't punish marital rape) and, most importantly, giving birth to sons to carry on the husband's family name. In addition, a respectable wife should bring stable income to the family. There is much complaining from male netizens that the traditional betrothal gift money (a euphemism for bride-price) has become too high, but this only proves men's eagerness for marriage rather than any inclination to abandon the system. They require such traditions to guarantee secure access to women, a concern similar to food security—female bodies are national resources.

Some terms have ignited controversy among women. "Donkey" or "donkey of marriage" (婚驴) suggests that married women are loyal and tame for domestic exploitation and hold antagonism toward single women. "Donkey of marriage" usually refers to married women who, numb to exploitation of themselves and other women, attack single women and especially scold their feminist daughters. The term fits into the context of everyday life so well that it does not appear to attack married women but rather to identify a common type of women in feminists' lives. The anger the term has aroused just proves that the exploitation and oppression that it implies do exist: "The reason the term 'donkey of marriage' has aroused so much rage is beyond the rhetoric itself but lies in the fact that it reveals truths behind the myth of marriage and the powerless state of married women" (EleanorSforza 2020).

Feminists are also criticized for such terms as *guonan* (蝈蝻), a homophone for "Chinese men" (国男) that uses characters for worm, and *qu* (蛆), maggot, which refers to anti-feminist males. Qin Liwen, a former senior journalist who now considers herself a Weibo feminist, expressed her opinion about the terms during an interview:

> From law, culture, and historical narration to everyday debates, women's disadvantage is obvious, as they are subjected to daily harassment and even massacre. All the angry words are pale compared to the reality we face us. I don't think there's any problem with the terms. Would the usual, peaceful discourse arouse any reaction? You must enrage your opponents and the so-called good citizens of society, showing them the ugliness under their noses and that they are accomplices by pretending not to see anything wrong.[7]

In their struggle to self-define, feminists stand by those being labelled and resist verbal violence by reinventing the labels themselves. This is similar to what U.S. feminists have done with terms such as "dyke" and "slut," though Chinese feminists have made this a more central practice. One prominent example is *tian yuan* (田园), an online term initially created to stigmatize feminists. Literally meaning "farmland" or "garden," *tian yuan* implies rural, uncivil, and unreasonable women arguing with men for money but refusing to take any responsibility (although no one has clarified exactly which responsibilities women have ever failed to take).[8] As an antonym of "*tian yuan* feminists," the so-called real feminists (真女权) are just another version of male-defined virtuous women. Refusing men's definitions and divisions of women, Chinese feminists all call themselves *tian yuan* (田园). They even use this term to protest inequality in farmland and homestead distribution in rural regions. A feminist program on Ximalaya FM, the leading podcast platform in China, is also called *you dian tian yuan* (有点田园), translated as "Into the Fields."

Today, farmlands and homesteads are collectively owned by villages in China and distributed (usually every thirty years) to villagers' families to manage by the household contract responsibility system (家庭联产承包责任制). As households are based on patrilocal residence and patrilineal family names, daughters earn less farmland for the family and almost no independent homesteads. Over the past forty years, the rise of capitalism has worsened the gender wealth gap in China's rural regions. Women, especially married daughters and their children, are often deprived of resettlement and land expropriation compensation and other village welfare initiatives such as education and travel subsidies (Li Huiying 2019). Weibo feminist account Catchup Gender-Equal Sisters (性别平等姐妹) created a tag for Li Huiying's book on the widening of the gender wealth gap in rural areas, promoting discussion on this topic. *Tian yuan* was successfully changed from an insult to the protesting watchword under which feminists unify.

After *tian yuan* fully lost its offensive implications, nü quan (女拳) came up. In Chinese, rights (权) and fist (拳) are homophones ("women's rights" and "women's fists" sound exactly the same). By calling feminists *quan shi* (拳师) (boxing masters), the opponents of feminists seek to humiliate them as aggressive and unattractive to men. However, enjoying the strength implied by the term, feminists took charge of these words, calling their feminist advocacy on Weibo their "daily boxing exercise" (每日打拳). For International Women's Day (March 8) 2020, a feminist artist drew and posted a picture of

Zhang Weili (the first Chinese woman to win the Ultimate Fighting Championship) under her Weibo account NLGSL. A very clear slogan says, "March 8 Women's Fists Day. Women Boxing Together," and a sentence at the bottom says, "Don't fear stigmatization. Speak out for women's rights." Zhang boxes against a background of vague words such as, "You are not a real feminist," or (on a politically charged topic), "The Feminist Five were arrested in 2015."[9]

Words and what they Carry

As solo carrier of a long and unique civilization, the Chinese language is powerful and tyrannical to its female readers. Chinese characters represent historical events and literary classics interwoven, encoding thousands of years' reality into a continuous patriarchal context. Every character is by itself a history, as the basic structures of Chinese characters were formed in oracle bone inscriptions over three thousand years ago and evolved into today's forms. Many characters convey misogyny and the subservient image of women in a picturesque way. The character of woman (女) seems to take a crooked and kneeling shape, since in oracle bone inscriptions it is ⏁ or ⏂. Slave (奴), adultery or rape (奸), and envy (嫉妒) all contain this component. Historical texts and literary texts are often seen as complementing each other, and the distinction between them is often unreliable. Hayden White (1973) emphasizes "the processes of selection and arrangement of data" in preparing chronicles. Events are reconstructed into a plausible story consisting of inaugural, transitional, and terminal events through a mode of emplotment, argument, and ideological implication (5–7).

In China, the selection and arrangement began at least 2,500 years ago when Confucius compiled historical materials into *Spring and Autumn* (春秋) through much interpretation and deletion.

Confucianism was a driving force in the historical accounts we have today. Confucian historians, who were also poets or essayists, openly announce the educative and ideological goals of their writings. The dominance of patriarchal histories comes not only from their orthodox status but also from their wide and deep absorption into language, culture, and everyday life. Even the most rudimentary users of Chinese usually gain some knowledge of historical proverbs (*cheng yu*/成语) and allusions (*dian gu*/典故). Any learner of the language is also incorporating millennia of legends of emperors and warlords. The selection, constant quotation, and mutual construction accumulate into a thick canon of male writings—a rigorous and confined context in which women's appearance, needs, and thoughts are simplified and stereotypical, and in which every artistic touch has sexism running through it.

This cultural context is both intimate and alienating to Chinese women. Turning to discourse of the Western, modern, or universal might appear to be a viable alternative. However, public discussions, dominated by government propaganda, have already turned "the universal" into a derogatory term. Furthermore, such discourse tends to be foreign, remote, and colonizing.

Lin Maomao (林毛毛), probably the most influential advocate for women-centered lifestyles on Weibo, was born in Tianjin, China, but now resides in Germany. She announced that she hadn't and never would teach her two daughters any Chinese, because the misogynistic pollutants in it can by no means be filtered. She chose to name her daughters with the surname of her German husband, to "bathe them fully in white," as she joked. She herself uses the language with sharp, witty, and powerful prose that attracted over 900,000 followers on Weibo. She has not given up on her country of birth even now that she is exiled from China's cyberspace.

Like Lin Yihan, Lin Maomao experienced trauma with the language before being able to see through the hostile trap in every character.

From enduring to criticizing, twisting violent characters into a means of self-expression—such is the epic experience of a Chinese woman writer, so severe that a mother would not want her daughters to suffer through it. Her rebellion and revenge is to cut off the inheritance of her language and her culture, which also means abandoning part of herself. Her daughters will probably never understand the brilliant words written by their mother, nor the inspiration she has brought to her readers.

In contrast to this cultural uprooting, other feminists have decided to construct a new context. They refuse to give the representative seat of their ethnic culture to men. Their collective effort involves tracing back to an earlier matrilineal civilization through characters and marginal anti-Confucian ancient texts. They support contemporary Chinese female writers too, urging them to write about female lives. Their recognition of women's writings surpasses nationality and ethnic identity to those outside mainland China, promoting the translation of women's writings from their original languages into Chinese—including many texts not yet translated into English. Translation and reintroduction broaden the resources and contexts of the Chinese language.

Closing the Gap Through Matrilineal Revival

Weibo feminists recognize the oppression built into the Chinese language but also excavate empowering facets. Etymology unveils matrilineal origin in Chinese culture, as *xing* (姓), meaning surname, signifies woman (女) plus birth (生), manifesting that surnames were originally passed down through the mother's lineage. Furthermore, the "eight main surnames from remote ancient times" (上古八大姓) all contain the woman (女) component, for example Ji (姬), Jiang (姜), Ying (嬴), and Yao (姚); they are at the origin of most surnames used today. This provides feminists with historical support to advocate that children bear the surnames of their mothers and call for women to fight for this right. Opponents argue that the mother's surname is also from her father, but according to the history of characters, her father's surname could ultimately trace back to a distant foremother.

Women need to battle against overwhelming obstacles to grant children their own surnames, though there is technically no law against it. Registering the names of newborn babies requires the presence of both parents. In one case, a man launched a lawsuit to divorce his wife because their son bore the mother's surname; after he divorced and won custody of the son, he resorted to law once again because this ex-wife still refused to change their son's surname to his. The court judged that the ex-wife needed to pay 100,000 yuan (around $14,000) to the man as compensation (*Hangzhou Daily* 2020). Such compensation is not granted to women, although over 90 percent of children bear their fathers' surnames.[10]

Divorced mothers are not allowed to change the surnames of the children they raise without their ex-husbands' permission, even when the ex-husbands don't pay child support. On Weibo, there is a super-chat (超话) called Purple-Ribbon Mother, for women whose children have been taken and hidden from them by the fathers' families. Many children were under two years old when taken away and have not seen their mothers since. The hegemony of surnames indicating that offspring belong to men and patriarchal families can easily stretch from the symbolic level to the actual deprivation of custody for mothers.

Indeed, the use of mothers' surnames is not only symbolic; it would be of immediate benefit in preventing abortion of female fetuses and entitling women to inheritance rights and increased financial support from their parents (lessening the gender wealth gap). The hegemony of surnames is at the core of Chinese patriarchy and contributes to the severely unbalanced sex ratio: 113.9 males per 100 females between 0 and 4 years old, and over 118 between 5 to 19 years old in 2018.[11] In a 2011 joint program of the United Nations Population Fund and China to reduce this gap, Changfeng county in Anhui province made policies giving families whose children bear the mother's surname financial rewards.[12] The policy soon aroused criticism from official media,[13] although such a fragmented reformation at a county level was probably little threat to the overall tradition. Millions of potential female lives have been lost, yet the problem is only raised when the surplus men are unable to find wives. Then, women are blamed for the impertinence of delaying marriage or staying single.

Behind the religious-like cult of continuing the patriarchal ancestral line, there is a whole set of economic interests and social mechanisms resulting from a settled agricultural society. Farmland, real estate, family savings, and especially human resources are organized based on patriarchal-family productive units built by marriage. The hegemony of surnames serves to guarantee the centralization of resources within patriarchal families. In this sense, marriage is a mechanism to guarantee men's possession of offspring (human resources), which is of even more economic, social, and cultural significance than of biological significance; parents would rather invest in adopted sons or nephews than in their own daughters. The argument over surnames shakes the fundamental structures of Chinese patriarchy. A blogger Writing Papers While Boxing (论文与打拳可以得兼) shared her own experience on Weibo: She divorced her husband because he refused to change their son's surname to hers, and raised much debate within and beyond feminist circles; the politics behind surnames was called to public attention. Soon after, her account was deleted by censors.

In addition to characters' etymologies, feminists pay much attention to pre- and anti-Confucian texts from ancient times. Some related discussions can be found under super-chats such as Matrilineal Societies Studies, Photographic Records of Single Women's Lives

(不婚女生活图鉴) and Loving-Women Literature (爱女文学), but most of them are scattered around the huge body of posts on Weibo. They are constantly disappearing due to censorship, which adds to the difficulty of finding materials in an already fragmented field.

Despite such obstacles, feminists on Weibo gather and discuss scattered historical records and literary studies of ancient texts that prove that women previously enjoyed political power as well as freedom in their private lives. Fu Hao (妇好), a female military leader and priestess from the Shang dynasty (over 3,000 years ago) is known to contemporary Chinese people since the discovery of her tomb in 1976. Feminist bloggers oppose the mainstream citing of this historical figure mainly as the wife of Wu Ding (武丁), the Shang dynasty emperor. Having her own independent fief and official title, which she passed down to her daughter with her own surname, Fu Hao is part of a huge matrilineal history. Fu Hao is also known as Hou Mu Xin (后母辛), Empress Mother Xin. Although in later history the character hou (后) means the spouse of a male ruler, in Fu Hao's time it probably meant a female ruler equal to the emperor. Feminists also pay much attention to the free lifestyles of women depicted in *Shi Jing* (诗经), or *Book of Songs*, a compilation of folk songs and poems from 11 B.C. to 6 B.C.

Taoism is the best-known counter-Confucian philosophy from ancient China. The earliest and the most important Taoist classic, *Tao Te Ching* (道德经), conveys matriarchal thinking in its explanation of how the universe formed and functions. It extols dialectics of nature and advocates for complying with nature in private and political life, going against the essentialism and absoluteness of hierarchal orders in Confucianism. It openly eulogizes the female genitals as the gate of eternal life and the root of the universe (in paragraph 6), which James Legge (1891) translates as:

The valley spirit dies not, aye the same,/谷神不死
The female mystery thus do we name./是谓玄牝
Its gate, from which at first they issued forth,/玄牝之门

Is called the root from which grew heaven and earth./是谓天地根
Long and unbroken does its power remain,/绵绵若存
Used gently, without the touch of pain./用之不勤

The vulva is translated as *xuan pin* (玄牝) (mysterious femaleness) and deified as *gu shen* (谷神), which James Legge translated as "valley spirit;" it could also be translated as "deity of crops" or "material abundance;" however, the image of the character 谷 (the labia spread, and a form is birthed) exhibits itself quite vividly. Some feminists joke that Lao Zi (老子) is in truth its homophone Lao Zi (姥子), maternal grandmother.

The unearthing of gynocentric traditions is not limited to mainstream or Han Chinese culture. Field studies and TV reports about China's matrilineal minority, the Mosuo (摩梭人), are often done by feminists, including interviews with Mosuo women who enjoy autonomy and independence and refuse to be regarded as someone's wife. A feminist account Strong Peaceful Bad Woman, which has been blocked, posted a series of readings and comments on the history of powerful matriarchs under the tag "The Last Mongolian Queens" (最后的蒙古女王). These discussions give voice to minorities rarely heard in mainstream Chinese media except in stereotypical propaganda (the recent musical "Wings of Songs" about the Uyghur minority is a typical example[14]). Weibo feminists are especially interested in minority women's voices, left out of the polemic with the United States on China's treatment of minorities, although the U.S. does not have a favorable record of justice toward its own minorities, for example the mass incarceration of African Americans mostly for non-violent offenses. Without entering such debates, feminists tend to approach minority cultures from an equal position rather than viewing them as exotic novelties. They present the vast possibilities of female and male lives across times and places.

Retrieving Lost Treasures in Literature

Although largely deprived of opportunities to write during one of the longest patriarchal histories in the world, Chinese women quickly gained lost ground in literature. Names of female writers such as Ding Ling (1904–1986), Xiao Hong (1911–1942), Eileen Zhang (1920–1995), Zhang Jie (1937–), Can Xue (1953–), Wang Anyi (1954–), and Chi Zijian (1964–) are at least as prominent as their male counterparts in the modern history of Chinese literature. Women blazed a path into literature with compelling and rigorous stories, breaking new ground with their themes and techniques. Their rapid progress is evident in laureates of the Mao Dun Literature Prize (茅盾文学奖), China's most prestigious award for writers.

Every four years, twenty-seven novels published between 1982 and 2007 were chosen, ten of which were by female authors. For the third (1985–1988) and fourth (1995–1998) awards, female writers were half the total winners. However, there have been no female winners of the past three awards (2007–2015), reflecting the worsening of women's status. Autonomous expression of women is difficult to coordinate with the government's increasingly nationalist agenda. Women's online literature, however, is thriving. Women's writings are massively encouraged and supported by other women, a clear example being Fang Fang and her diaries.

While Wuhan was under lockdown due to the COVID-19 pandemic from January to April 2020, the local female writer Fang Fang (方方) wrote and published her diaries online. These incurred attacks from government supporters. When her diaries were first published abroad in English as *Wuhan Diary: Dispatches from the Original Epicenter* (Fang Fang 2020), the author suffered much cyber violence calling her a traitor to her country. Yu Xiuhua (余秀华), a disabled female poet, is among the few in literary circles who openly supported Fang Fang: "An individual's sorrow should not be censored."[15] (Yu Xiuhua 2020). Although the original post has been blocked, feminist account Her History2 reposted Yu's article in pictures, a widespread feminist tactic to avoid censorship. Having suffered forced marriage, domestic violence, and unequal terms for divorce as a disabled rural woman before she won recognition for her poems, Yu Xiuhua has received massive support since feminist account Chengyusan introduced her story and protested the injustice of her divorce case in 2016.

In addition to the representation of female writers, feminists focus on the bias against women in literature, including in some women's writings. They criticize female writers catering to male-defined literary traditions rather than voicing the problems in women's lives:

> Women can't face up to their sex and women's history stretching from remote ancient times to today; they can't stick to women's ultimate concerns. It illustrates the self-contempt and avoidance of their identity deeply ingrained in many women's hearts ... Many female writers have chosen topics unrelated to women deliberately ... turning to "broader" and "more miscellaneous" themes and realms of stories, hiding their selves and even the whole female group to manifest "transgression" of their gender ... She is not only transgressing her gender, but her time, her past and present.
>
> Liu 1995, 205

Dan mei (耽美), literally "indulging in beauty," is a popular genre created by and for women about homosexual male romance. It has become a hot topic among feminists. Why are so many women and girls interested in or even crazy about gay love? *Dan mei* novels and stories offer a huge and complex array of themes and perspectives, making it difficult to give a simple conclusion about its merits or faults for feminist agendas.

It is clear, however, that *dan mei*'s popularity and commercial success in television adaptations are rooted in patriarchal cultural domination. Women eulogize idealized love between males, and this has been the most tolerated women-created genre in censor-ridden China, though there is no guarantee that it will not be targeted in the future by the unpredictable censors. Unlike lesbian or feminist culture that bring about a loss of obedient reproductive tools for the nation, love among men is more acceptable to the authorities. It does not affect birth rate, as most gay men are in the closet and marry women, and an increasing number use surrogates. *Dan mei* is a cathartic way for women to escape a heterosexual culture that instrumentalizes female bodies and identify with the egalitarian romantic portrayals of men.

Figure 5.1 Poster of a very famous TV drama adapted from *dan mei* Literature. The male protagonists are predominant on the posters, women marginalized or even not shown on the posters. The homosexual love is reworded as brotherhood in the drama to bypass the governmental census, though it is fully implied in the plots. "Guardian" directed by Zhou Yuanzhou © 时悦影视 2018. All right reserved.

Gay male romances are used by women to depict the empathetic love that they long for. By identifying with one of the male lovers or worshipping both beautiful heroes, women meet their ideal of humane relations without the degradation and shame that heterosexuality imposes on women. Often the protagonists are unrealistically elevated by their affectionate female creators.

Appealing to facets of female desire in an unobtainable way, *dan mei* inevitably marginalizes women in cultural products; and again women's talent is recognized only when they use it to eulogize and idealize men. The prevailing *dan mei* culture creates beautiful homosexual men—male gods for women to worship in the rigid context of heteropatriarchy. This is relevant to what Mary Daly (1990) has observed about the mythic archetypes Dionysus and Apollo. While the super-masculine Apollo maintains and dignifies the essential patriarchal orders, the feminine Dionysus drives women to the loss of self in a pleasure-taking emotional catharsis, as a complement to the rigidity of Apollo:

> Madness is the only ecstasy offered to women by the Dionysian way ... While the supermasculine Apollo overtly oppresses/ destroys with his contrived boundaries/hierarchies/rules/roles, the feminine Dionysus blurs the senses, confuses his victims—drugging them into complicity ... The rituals of romantic love as well as those of religion draw women into the "ecstasy" of Self-loss.
>
> 66–67

Feminists on Weibo have sensed this female annihilation in popular culture and launched forceful criticism of it. In 2019, Weibo blogger LOSTINUR_ParaN (2020) posted statistics about TV shows in China. Only 19.8 percent used women as protagonists and in 41 percent of TV shows, actresses made up less than 30 percent of the total cast, while 24.3 percent of all shows feature dual male protagonists, some adapted from *dan mei* novels (almost none feature dual female protagonists). With the rise of TV shows adapted from *dan mei* novels, the number of female actresses and pop stars on screen has decreased dramatically, with their commercial value and social influence declining. Many feminist bloggers point out the self-deceiving "consuming of the male body" (消费男色) including money spent by girls and women to support their male idols: "The disappearance of female stars from the screen drives women into dead ends in all social and public places," a feminist blogger Her History2 commented under a post titled, "Almost all male stars for TV shows."[16] Another feminist blogger Cat With A Lighter (2020) observed, "It is poisoning to the construction of women's selves, because all the ideal personalities could only be cast in male bodies." This female-erasing ethos is similar to the masculinized Iron Girl image used during Mao's era, as "Iron Girl" could contribute to the industrialization of China through forsaking any difference from men. While never getting equal pay for equal work, women's personal emotions were repressed and they even couldn't choose who to marry (Zhou and Guo 2013, 7–8). Women were encouraged to identify with male bodies as their only source of strength, pride (and now even fantasies of love), and to not notice they are deprived of the equal rights.

Feminists urge female writers to write about and for women, and they support independent voices amid the dominant discourse of nationalism both in popular culture and in "serious literature." Under the super-chat Loving-Women Literature (爱女文学), there are recommendations and discussions for online novels that present healthy and natural images of women, including lesbians.

The enthusiasm for seeing female lives and experiences in literature and the keen following of new books by various feminist accounts on Weibo have promoted the translation and introduction of a global feminist corpus in China. As previously mentioned, *Fang Siqi's First Love Paradise* by Taiwanese writer Lin Yihan enjoyed a warm welcome in mainland China's book market in spite of the cold political relations between Taiwan and mainland China. Japanese journalist Shiori Itō's account of being raped, *Black Box,* and Japanese feminist Chizuko Ueno's *Misogyny in Japan* (厌女: 日本的女性嫌恶) are also popular in their Chinese translations (incidentally, English translations do not exist). A current popular book series among Weibo feminists is Italian female writer Elena Ferrante's *Neapolitan Novels.* In the digital world of Weibo, by following feminist posts and reposts, readers can find global women's literature ranging from poems of Korean modern female poet Moon Jung Hee (문정희) to the introduction of the newly published French novel *Le Consentement,* although the latter has not yet been translated into Chinese.

From the ancient to the contemporary, and to the translated, feminists' tracing back and digging up of historical texts and women's writings provide a presence of female-centered narratives on Weibo. However, feeling that this presence is still not strong and radical enough to resist the current surge of nationalist patriarchal discourse, feminists pick up their pens to create what they believe women's literature should be.

Feminist Literary Creations on Weibo

Literary writing of feminists on Weibo is an autonomous and mostly non-profit activity done out of enthusiasm for self-expression. The writings are circulated online through feminist accounts or super-chats. An account Sisters' Editorial Office (姐妹编辑部), run by volunteers, reposts poems, essays, short stories, and novellas that take a feminist stance; under the super-chat No. 91 Hou De Li (厚德里91号) (an address in Shanghai where pioneering feminist Qiu Jin/秋瑾 [1875–1907] lived), many feminist creative writings accumulate. The majority of these writings are self-narrating or confessional prose, feminist utopian and dystopian stories, and rewritings of mythologies or fantasies.

Responding to the call for reversion to women-centered narratives, many Chinese women write their personal experiences, often traumatic, into confessional prose. The content varies from childhood sexual abuse and disputes with parents to personal experiences of becoming feminists and constructing a body of Chinese women's documentary literature on Weibo. Through literary writings, feminists maintain a mild but persistent movement akin to Me Too, which was suppressed by Chinese authorities when the Western movement caught on in China in 2017. The strong, empathetic, and rebellious words of women distinguish their writings from the sympathetic and pitiable texts about women of male authors such as Lu Xun, who "write on the corpse of women," as Lydia Liu (1995) has noted. Both personal and political, the writings function as therapy and identity construction, similar to what bell hooks has described: "It emerges as a narrative of resistance, as writing that enables us to experience both self-discovery and self-recovery" (5).

Ma Panyan (马泮艳), born in 1988, shares her experiences on Weibo under the name Wushan Liu Yue Xue (巫山六月雪). Wushan (巫山), near the world-famous Three Gorges on the Yangzi River, is her hometown, while Liu Yue Xue (六月雪), "snow of June," has a specific meaning in China. It is said that if someone has been severely wronged by society, and justice on earth failed to come forth, there will be snow in June to send rage and punishment from heaven. Kept in captivity, brutally abused for years and having given birth to two children, she finally managed to escape and become a migrant worker. When she planned to register marriage with her new boyfriend, she was astonished to be told that she was already married, though she had never signed any documents. Although Ma gave birth to her eldest daughter at the age of 14, the lowest age for sexual consent in China, and her story drew much public attention after being reported by the media, neither her "ex-husband" who had raped her nor the relatives who had sold her at age twelve as child bride have ever been arrested. Ma, who received almost no schooling, has now learned to write. Sketching past scenes with brief, clear-cut, and vivid language, she records both crimes and slight kindnesses that came her way. Resorting to writing as a means to gain justice, she is not waiting for the snow of June; she has become it:

> A crowd of people sat in circle on the living room of my fourth aunt's husband; they were there to negotiate the selling of me. Second aunt and her husband, two female cousins, third aunt, the elder brother of fourth aunt's husband—they were all present . . . They urged me to agree to marry Chen Xuesheng. I shook my head, saying I didn't agree. They pretended not to hear. When I repeated it, fourth aunt's husband came forth and slapped my face twice. This shadowy crowd of relatives stared at my face like wolves, expecting me, a 12-year-old, to say yes as soon as possible, so they could go to bed.
>
> Ma, *My Own Experiences V*, 2020, para. 8

Ma's writing not only narrates her sufferings but also reveals a broader feminist awareness of the exploitative nature of marriage. She vividly describes reactions in the remote village of Wushan after her mother, who suffered from a mental disorder, killed her father after being abused for years:

> My sister and I were terrified, crying aloud. My eldest uncle (father's elder brother) heard it; he just stood by his door staring at us coldly . . . Before the police came to my home, there were already many neighbors gathering to watch. A nearby neighbor pushed my mother down to kneel on a bench, slapping her face hard several times until she lost consciousness. The village leaders cut two bamboo sticks, thick and wide. After dumping water on my mother to force her to kneel down, they beat her with bamboo . . . Then, they and my eldest uncle ordered my mother to carry my father's body back from the farm. Although there was a long upward slope from the farmland to our house, my mother, wounded all over, carried my father back without a break . . . Later, after inspection,

the police handcuffed and drew my mother away with a rope tied
around her waist . . . The village leaders and eldest uncle sold all our
fat pigs—for my father's coffin, they said. The chickens left were
caught for dinner by the village leaders.

                    Ma, *My Own Experiences I*, 2020, para. 4–6

From officials to ordinary villagers, all were absorbed in punishing
the woman immediately and watching, while the dead body was left
lying on the farmland. The punishment emphasizes the humiliation
and beating down of the female body, to kill her identity as a member
of society. Her true crime was violation of patriarchal ethics by killing
her husband, her master, more than the murder itself. The police drew
her away with a rope, degrading her to animal status.

Behind the set of ritual and ethical judgements, patriarchal
ownership of farmlands and real estate and distribution of assets
reveals itself. Through expelling Ma's mother from the village, the
relatives split and occupy the family's farmland. As for the three
orphan daughters, their inheritance right was cancelled through
marriage; they were sent out as child brides one by one. Similar to
witch-hunting in medieval Europe, under the cover of patriarchal
religious or ethical excuses, single, independent, or rebellious women
in China are regularly robbed of their assets.

In addition to memoirs of sociopolitical significance, a prevalent
genre of Weibo literature is feminist utopia/dystopia. One predominant
feature is that, rather than "construct ideal space in order to subvert
inequality and inevitability" and "dislocate historical determinism"
(Pfaelzer 1988, 228), the writers describe extreme patriarchal societies
and the process of overthrowing them. The ideal feminist utopian
society is sketched briefly as the final victory and promised future, but
the writers (and readers) are mainly concerned with scrutinizing the
mechanisms of patriarchy and eulogizing rebellions and struggles
under the most desperate circumstances. The created world, whether
utopia or dystopia, could only be understood in reference to current

circumstances. Sharp confrontations between the sexes in literary writings reflect the keen anxiety of Chinese feminists in a society that is more and more hostile to women, and also their firm determination to rebel. For both writers and readers, the writings function as a methodology to scrutinize the patriarchal mechanism that they struggle against in reality and support their struggles with the final realization of justice in literature.

The World of Uterus (*Fengxing*, 2020) compiles fictional news reports, law excerpts, and magazine articles to present an extreme patriarchal world following the genocide of women and the invention of the artificial uterus for procreation, and finally the collapse of the patriarchal republic. There are laws such as the Crime of Being Women (女罪法), a newspaper article, "Ten Thousand Men's Revelry: Masculinity Purifies the Fortress of Human Beings" in *Penis Daily* and the heading, "Anniversary of Victory Day—War Proved Man Is the Ruler of the World" on *Purging Earth News*. With a tone typical of real-world propaganda, this sounds like official daily news broadcasting. It is the reality, not the story, that is absurd and terrifying.

Another sci-fi novella, "Gause's Law: After Man-Made Uterus" (高斯定理：人造子宫发明后会怎样) by Siye (2019) focuses on women's rebellion. After nuclear war and female genocide, men created a single-sex hierarchal republic and used biological technology to change women to "subhumans" in breeding centers. They cannot walk straight because of twisted spines and their awareness is kept at the level of ten-year-olds. Every man can be allotted a subhuman to serve him and bear his children, although most men are also controlled from a higher level, forced to eat white tablets at certain intervals to keep them tame.

Eight underground female habitations were built by female scientists led by Wa (娲) as shelters before the nuclear war. Wa is named after the highest goddess in Chinese mythology, who created human beings with earth as miniatures of herself and mended the broken sky to save people from a flood. Pretending to be a man, this contemporary Wa spies on the central lab of the republic. Her underground army destroys it, liberating all subhumans. This implies that even in situations most hostile to women, there are feminists ready and able to fight.

The rewriting of myth and fantasy by feminists helps to reverse mythological archetypes. For example, mainstream versions of Greek myths dramatize stereotypical jealousy, competition, and persecution among women. But in "Song of Siren" (塞壬之歌) by Cha An (2019), the writer reverses the plot so that women protect each other from men. Siren and Muse are close friends. Zeus is attracted by the beautiful wings of Siren. Seeing Zeus coming with fetters to lock up Siren, Muse pretends to be jealous and removes Siren's wings with great sorrow. Siren is set free despite her loss, but Muse is kept in confinement by Zeus for ruining his sexual hunting. Seeing Siren killed by Odysseus through a mirror, Muse's soul collapses into nine. The difficulties and determinations of female friendship in an authoritarian, male-dominated context are made clear through this mythic revision, as are the cover-ups and false interpretations of events that slander women. Women do what they can to survive and protect one another under the most oppressive conditions. Earlier stories such as Ling Shuhua's "Once Upon a Time" (1928) and Wang Anyi's "Brothers" (1989) are also about sisterhood and romance between women that ultimately cannot survive the crushing tide of patriarchal social norms. In *The Emerging Lesbian*, Sang Tze-lang traces the history of intimacy between Chinese women for centuries and ties it with China's social and cultural evolution. Lesbianism, she suggests, was a prominent theme during the modernizing of China and represented a rise in women's status, though it was typically portrayed as ceding to patriarchal requirements. Weibo feminists continue the tradition of presenting desirable Sapphic love.

Wuxia (martial arts literature) is a typical Chinese genre that has widespread influence and is traditionally highly misogynistic. Though always present, female warriors are misrepresented and used as tools for men's plans. However, today's female authors are revising this genre. "Opposite Camps?" (正邪不两立) by Junzi (2019) satirizes a typical male plot pattern in Wuxia, where a female warrior (*nü xia/* 女侠) falls in love with a dissolute man after he saw her body or sexually harassed her. Jun's story describes the lesbian love between two female warriors who defy arrogant male illusions of conquering women. As embodiments of Chinese professional women, female warriors' role has been restored in the fight against being othered by phallocratic language, redefining the female warrior archetype.

With these writings, feminists construct their own cultural community in the digital world. They refuse self-repression and kick away the shadow of potential male readers in their minds. This free flowing of women's creativity has been constantly hindered, however, by government authorities. The censorship and anti-pornography campaign (扫黄) is biased against women. Jin Jiang, the largest female-oriented online literature site, was completely shut down by censors in May, 2019. When it reopened, users found many chapters of novels finished years ago unavailable. It appears that any physical descriptions below the neck written by women are automatically blocked. Today's version is more extreme than the censorship or exploitation of women's sensuality from literature by female writers such as Ding Ling, Lin Bai, and Chen Ran in the 1920s and 1990s (Kong 2004; Ferry 2018). In March 2020, many Chinese women suffered from the censorship of ao3 (Archive of Our Own). While empowering physical descriptions by women are censored, pornographic pop-ups still constantly jump to the screen of any Chinese internet user (including children), exhibiting female bodies as sex toys (though with key parts covered). These are very hard for individual users to block, if not impossible, and unthinkable in the U.S., as they are omnipresent in many webpages and advertisements bound with the programs installed in the computer.

As a place to circulate scattered news and ideas, Weibo is unable to draw wide readership to feminist creative writers, let alone earn economic benefits for them. Most of these writings are destined to be lost in the mass of fragmented, shallow digital information. It is an even worse place for poetry than for science fiction. However, blogger Qunxing (2020) has posted several of her poems on Weibo, and one poem "Her Poetic Era" (她的诗纪) discusses the tenuous future of women's writing itself. It contains deliberate deletion, negation, and forgetting. The poem foresees its own oblivion: "Heading to death/I suddenly began to write a poem" and "I chose to be forgotten/ But being forgotten brings no forgiveness of me."[17] She is writing out of the refusal to forgive the world's parasitism of the "nameless women," from the first one to herself. Like other feminist creative writings on Weibo, this is a battling literature, a struggling expression, and therefore only in a future when women's status has been restored will the destructive poems of nameless women finally cease to be, transcending a constructive language as the poet longs to do: "My poem dies and revives in her era."[18]

Works Cited

Cat With A Lighter [@拿打火机的猫]. (2020, April 27). 为什么 "消费" 男色并不女权 [Why "Consuming Male Bodies" Is Not Feminism] Weibo. https://weibo.com/6816655437/IFhv7zrx2?type=comment.

Cha An [@茶安_2018]. (2019, August 3). 塞壬之歌 [Song of Siren]. Weibo. https://weibo.com/ttarticle/p/show?id=2309404401183199461385.

Chengyusan [@橙雨伞微博]. (2016, August 1). 余秀华离掉包办婚姻, 为何还要给前夫精神损失费？ [Divorcing Her Husband after Forced Marriage, Why Did Yu Xiuhua Still Need to Pay Her Ex Mental Damage Compensation?]. Weibo. https://weibo.com/ttarticle/p/show?id=2309404003611758728840#_0.

Daly, Mary (1990). *Gyn/Ecology: The Metaethics of Radical Feminism*. Beacon Press.

EleanorSforza [@EleanorSforza]. (2020, May 15). 让我难过的是 [What Makes Sad]. Weibo. https://weibo.com/3852516814/J202WjGk4?display= 0&retcode=6102&type=comment.

Fang Fang. (2020). *Wuhan Diary: Dispatches from a Quarantined City.* (M. Berry, Trans.). Harper Collins Publishers.

Fengxing [@风行无叶]. (2020, March 27). 尤忒瑞斯的世界 [The World of Uterus]. Weibo. https://m.weibo.cn/status/4486973785964136?.

Ferry, Megan (2018). *Chinese Women Writers and Modern Print Culture.* Cambria.

Hangzhou Daily [@杭州日报]. (2020, May 19). 夫妻俩离婚时约定孩子随父姓女方反悔 法院判决：女方支付违约金10万 [Woman Refuses to Change Child's Surname to the Father's after Divorce: Court Rules She Must Pay 100,000 Yuan]. Weibo. https://weibo.com/1644358851/ J2FwLt1Ho?type=comment#_rnd1590374279652.

Hong Fincher, Leta. (2014). *Leftover Women: The Resurgence of Gender Inequality in China.* Zed Books Ltd.

hooks, bell. (1999). *Remembered Rapture: The Writer at Work.* Henry Holt and Company.

Itō, Shiori. (2019). 黑箱 [*Black Box*]. (Kuang Kuang, trans.). CITIC Press Group. (Original work published 2017).

Junzi [@君子风寻]. (2019, September 22). 正邪不两立？ [Opposite Camps?] Weibo. https://weibo.com/ttarticle/p/show?id=2309404419301011488800.

Kong, Shuyu (2004). *Consuming Literature.* Stanford UP.

Lao Zi. *Dao De Jing.* (J. Legge, trans.). Chinese Text Project. https://ctext.org/ dao-de-jing/ens.

Li, Huiying. (2019). 乡村社会治理与性别分层加剧研究 [Research on Social Governance of Rural Areas and the Increasing Disparity between Genders]. China Social Science Press.

Lin Maomao [@林毛毛]. (2019). 说到我孩子的德语名随父姓 [About My Children Taking the German Surname of Their Father]. Weibo. https:// weibo.com/1671890613/HDjWw0gT7?type=comment.

Lin Yinhan. (2017, May 5). 这是关于《房思琪的初恋乐园》这部作品，我想对读者说的事情. [This Is What I Want to Say to Readers about *Fang Siqi's First Love Paradise*] [Interview]. Readmoo News. https://news. readmoo.com/2017/05/05/170505-interview-with-lin-02/.

Lin, Yihan. (2018). 房思琪的初恋乐园 [*Fang Siqi's First Love Paradise*]. Beijing United Publishing Co., Ltd.

Liu, Huiying. (1995). 走出男权传统的樊篱：文学中男权意识的批判 [Criticism of Patriarchal Ideology in Literature]. SDX Joint Publishing Company.

Liu, Lydia (1995). *Translingual Practices*. Stanford UP.

LOSTINUR_ParaN [@LOSTINUR_ParaN]. (2020, February 10). *2019 年中国大陆首播电视剧女性相关数据* [Statistics about TV Series First Released in 2019 in Mainland China]. Weibo. https://weibo.com/5036197947/ItzJPzS0X?type=comment#_rnd1588615169395.

Ma, Panyan [@巫山六月雪]. (2020, April 19). *我的亲身经历：旧事一* [*My Own Experiences: One*]. Weibo. https://weibo.com/ttarticle/p/show?id=2309404495564862521349#_0.

Ma, Panyan [@巫山六月雪]. (2020, April 25). *我的亲身经历：旧事五* [*My Own Experiences: Five*]. Weibo. https://weibo.com/ttarticle/p/show?id=2309404497542648824013#_0.

NLGSL [@NLGSL]. (2020, March 8). 3.8 女权节 [March 8 Women's Fists Day][Painting]. Weibo. https://weibo.com/6501758411/IxG9Pd3r2?from=page_1005056501758411_profile&wvr=6&mod=weibotime&type=comment#_rnd1590412460216.

Pfaelzer, Jean. (1988). The Changing of Avant Garde: The Feminist Utopia. *Science Fiction Studies*, 15(3), 282–294.

Qunxing [@群星诗纪]. (2020, January 6). 她的诗纪 [Her Poetic Era]. Weibo. https://s.weibo.com/weibo?q=她的诗纪&Refer=user_weibo.

Ruobing [若冰]. (2021, January 14). 《海马星球》覃里雯：我是如何进化为"女本位"的女权主义者 [Qin Liwen and Her Planet of Sea Horse: How Do I Evolve to a Female-centered Feminist]. The Paper. https://m.thepaper.cn/baijiahao_10762445.

Siye [@四叶重楼_貌似学霸心是渣]. (2020, July 25). 高斯定理：人造子宫发明后会怎样 [*Gause's Law: After Man-Made Uterus*]. Weibo. https://weibo.com/1897134231/HF7pnvsjm?type=comment#_rnd1588642950969.

White, Hayden. (1973). *Metahistory: The Historical Imagination in Nineteen Century Europe*. The Jones Hopkins University Press.

Wittig, Monique. (1992). *The Straight Mind and Other Essays*. Beacon Press.

Xu, Ruijuan. (2014). 永宁摩梭"母系"文化词群研究 [Matrilineal Language and Culture of Mosuo People of Yong Ning County]. The Ethnic Publishing House.

Yu, Xiuhua. (2020, April 13). 爱国贼和爱国奴：关于方方日记的一点小想法 [Traitors and Slaves in Name of Patriots: Some Thoughts on Fang Fang's Diary]. Weixin. https://mp.weixin.qq.com/s/dZ6Qpmw9ZBhPg9yqkk9ZZA.

Zhou, D. and Guo Y. (2013). "Gender, Power and Identity Construction – Taking Dazhai's "Iron Girls" as a Case". Nationalities Research in Qinghai, 24(1), 5–10.

"You Forbid Us to Gather Anywhere, So We Will be Everywhere:" Weibo Feminism as a Global Solution

Women in China are at an unprecedented time where dissemination of information has reached massive speed and volume. China has the world's largest population and Chinese is one of the world's most spoken languages, second only to English. This gives women access to an enormous public audience, made possible by the internet and notably the biggest online platform, Weibo. Feminist ideas have now reached a larger audience. While many men read and oppose them, a huge portion of ordinary women find truth in them and add their own voices.

Weibo feminism is a unique movement for the number of followers and the diversity of views across class and ethnic lines, representing a wide range of life experiences and education levels. This diversity is its strength, as it willfully and pridefully encompasses and incorporates all female experience. This makes it stand apart from some intellectual elite feminists, who are often mouthpieces of the State's propaganda machines. More and more ordinary people are questioning the government and ordinary women are questioning the equally powerful institution of the patriarchal family based on a tradition that was reified during Confucius' time.

Parallel to the rise of Weibo feminism, censorship and repression have also increased. Currently, the Chinese government has a nationalist and natalist agenda. It revoked the one-child policy due to concern over an aging population and is now actively encouraging women to give birth to two children and stigmatizing those who resist motherhood within marriage. Paradoxically, the push to provide offspring does not extend to single or lesbian women, and they are punished and ostracized in ways left over from the one-child policy.

Weibo feminists have responded with one of their usual tactics: reinventing and reclaiming terms. In this case, "womb morality" reverses the patriarchal moral judgments placed on women and states that true morality is sexual and reproductive freedom. This includes women's right to have children out of wedlock, selecting desirable genetic material from men without any commitment to them, as well as the right, even in marriage, to give children the mother's surname. Passing on surnames is a main justification for the preference for sons that has led to the most severe gender ratio imbalance in the world (mostly through selective abortions) and restriction of inheritance rights.

It is interesting to compare Weibo feminism to Western feminism. Doing so can shed light not only on the respective situations but also what the world can learn from Weibo feminism. It is not only influencing the largest population of any feminist movement but also contains lessons for feminists everywhere. Just as Weibo feminists are well-informed about the global situation, so the world deserves to know about them. More global alliances and sharing ideas among feminists corresponds with Weibo feminists' statement that all women's lives are intertwined. Together, women can locate the roots of patriarchy and pull them up, replanting their own histories in their rightful places.

Indeed, history is a major concern for Weibo feminists. Together, they reassemble prehistory and history – Chinese and global – that puts women in their places as empresses, queens, inventors, and major contributors to civilization who were intentionally erased. From archeology to etymology, Weibo feminists use every tool available to read between the official historical narratives' lines and to write and dig beyond them. This is especially important in China, where history is cited in everyday life and contributes to the unifying rhetoric that is the glue of society.

Significantly, feminist discussions are censored on Weibo to the extent that many feminist terms are considered sensitive words, and long blogs from feminist accounts, containing such words or not, are blocked immediately on being sent out or limited from spreading to a wide audience. Technologies such as computer algorithms become a primary weapon to control the public. Feminists have thus been forced to invest in every sphere of Weibo life. Although this government effort for dispersion intends to marginalize feminist concerns, it sometimes has the opposite effect. Through being refused their own space, feminists have learned to be everywhere. That has had a huge impact on public opinion and brought feminism into the mainstream. Although many argue against it, people who would never otherwise be interested in feminism are part of the discussion in huge numbers. When many men and some women offer bad-faith arguments and attacks, this often leads to more women seeing that the feminists are right.

During the writing of this book, we went through several disastrous censoring moments alongside Weibo feminists. Some of the sources cited in the book, such as the writings of Lin Maomao and Hou Hongbin, disappeared from all cyberspace in mainland China overnight. Lin betrays a plebeian irony, joking while piercing to the heart of the ugliness and deformation of traditional Chinese lives, while Hou, appearing more elitist, adopts an intellectual approach in her comments on social news and cultural products. Both are considered threats to be rid of, betraying the embedded fear of the ruling party. The authorities closed all the feminist-related chat groups on Danban and censored tags for lesbian novels on an online literature site, presaging that Weibo feminism, or Chinese feminism, is by no means on a smooth track. Still, whoever sees the vibrant creativity and uncompromising will of Chinese feminists will know that the movement will persist. Since you forbid us to gather anywhere, we feminists will be everywhere.

More than ever, women are fighting back and claiming their own creations and spaces. Just as magical realism in its Latin American origins was created to circumvent government censors who were uneducated and thought the stories fantastical escapes rather than political allegories, Chinese women write fiction set in ancient times to bring to light contemporary struggles. They also reinvent words and decolonize the Chinese language from its patriarchal control and use as a tool to violate women. Far from giving up on Chinese history, culture, and language, many reframe these with pride.

The COVID-19 pandemic further brought feminist concerns to the attention of the overall public. Feminists organized effective and transparent actions, for example getting menstrual products to frontline workers and calling attention to the vast majority of these being women. Chinese women have long enjoyed high rates of employment outside the home but receive scant representation at higher levels. They are also shackled with the burdens of unpaid care work still assumed to be their natural calling. Patriarchal families claim rights over women's reproductive systems especially to gain male heirs. More and more women realize this is fundamentally unequal and refuse to marry. They do not see the one-child policy's end as liberation but recognize instead new guises of patriarchal control emerging, especially with reproductive technologies and surrogacy.

Critical of both Chinese patriarchal tradition and Western ideological imperialism, Weibo feminists are creating a movement that is populist, feminist, distinctly Chinese, and beneficial to women everywhere. The insights of millions of women bravely and radically challenge patriarchal ruling mechanisms in their Confucian specificity and their global consistency, calling for women together to demission from patriarchal institutions on a personal level, which will make them crumble instantly. If all women see the commonality in their lives and support each other in this major divestment, a world of freedom and equality can emerge for all (women, children, and men). Indeed, feminist solutions to the world's problems are holistic and collaborative, a powerful antidote to tokenism and the patriarchal ethos of possession and competition.

While Western liberal feminism obscures many issues with a postmodern rhetoric of choice, Weibo feminists are grounded in the material realities of real women's lives. In the West, some "progressive" politics makes talking about women's oppression impossible, or at least unfashionable, since the category "women" is supposedly just a matter of personal choice. While second-wave feminists gained much ground through recognizing the commonality of women's experience and collectively fighting oppression and cultivating pride, the energies of the Western Left are now elsewhere. Weibo feminists, however, are a contemporary version of 1970s women's movements with both Chinese and global characteristics. The dominant (mediatized) liberal feminism in the West frames surrogacy, for example, as an issue of women's choice. Weibo feminists highlight how choice does not exist in a context wherein women have been deprived of reproductive rights for millennia. Although this might seem obvious in the Chinese context and specific to it, Weibo feminism invites all women to see that the specifics are a matter of degree and form, but the root issues are the same worldwide.

If anyone can point out contradictions and offer viable alternatives, it is Weibo feminists, with their massive collective talents for humor, art, literature, analysis, and grounding in real, shared experience of women striving to live beyond patriarchy in a global sisterhood. While it is tempting to blame problems on the specificity of China's one-party rule, or even that combined with its Confucian patriarchal legacy, Weibo feminists are critical of all patriarchal institutions. They caution against the mentality of "women are worse off over there, so we should be happy." The problems are similar, and only through women working together in empathy and solidarity can they be solved. We hope, by showing the courage and creativity of Weibo feminism to the world, this book is an inspiring step toward this goal.

Notes

Introduction Scattered revolutions spark the masses

1   According to the latest calculation by the Central Committee of China
    Communist Party, women constituted 28.8 percent of the total
    95,148,000 party members in China in June 2021. See https://
    news.12371.cn/dzybmbdj/zzb/dntjgb/. Only a few women hold
    high-level or ministerial positions in the government. See www.
    weforum.org/reports/global-gender-gap-report-2021.

2   The female to male ratio in higher education ranks first in the world
    while in secondary education ranks 124th. See Global Gender Gap
    Report, 2021 at www.weforum.org/reports/global-gender-gap-
    report-2021.

3   From Weibo Users Development Report 2020, issued by the Weibo
    official data center: https://data.weibo.com/report/reportDetail?id=456.

4   Ding, J. (1993). 毛泽东关于中国妇女解放道路的思想 [Mao Zedong's
    Thoughts on the Approach to Chinese Women's Emancipation]. *Journal
    of Chinese Women's Studies*, 04, 8–12.

5   Wesoky, S. R. (2016). Politics at the Local-Global Intersection: Meanings
    of Bentuhua and Transnational feminism in China. *Asian Studies
    Review*, 40(1), 53–69.
    Wang, Z. (1999). *Women in the Chinese Enlightenment: Oral and Textual
    Histories*. University of California Press.
    Wang, Z. (2005). "State Feminism?" Gender and Socialist State
    Formation in Maoist China. *Feminist Studies*, 31(3), pp. 519–551.
    Wang, Z. and Zhang, Y. (2010). Global Concepts, Local Practices:
    Chinese Feminism Since the Fourth UN Conference on Women.
    Feminist Studies, 36(1), pp. 40–70.

6   Represented by Lü Pin (吕频) and the Women's Voice (女权之声). For
    Weibo users who have publicized their real names or have renowned
    online pseudonyms, the real names or pseudonyms are used, and if not,
    we will use their Weibo username. For usernames too long and/or

containing non-verbal symbols, only the phonetic transcription of the first three characters will be preserved, while the corresponding full username in Chinese will be listed in the citation list.

7   Such as Muzimei (木子美), Queen Yiheng (女王易衡), and Ye Haiyan (叶海燕).
8   The early representatives include Baihuliuli (白虎琉璃) and Lin Maomao (林毛毛).
9   Hong Fincher, Leta (2018). *Betraying Big Brother: The Feminist Awakening in China*. Verso.
10 Such as Xianzi (弦子) and Shaoxi (稍息).
11 Such as Xiezilou (写字楼大妈), Guozili (果子狸), Shaoxi (稍息), Eyumaomao (鳄鱼毛毛), and Hou Hongbin (侯虹斌).

1   Feminist outbreaks in the digital world

1   According to the Global Gender Gap Report 2021 issued by the World Economic Forum (2021).
2   The data were publicized by the Foundation in its working reports of the first two seasons in 2020: www.hhax.org/nv.html?nid=ee8a5c49-47a0-4e7f-985b-cc698214a5d9.
3   姐妹战疫安心行动 (Chen C. 2020).
4   看见女性劳动者.
5   不仅此次医务人员需要，还有执行特殊任务的女警察 . . . 女消防员，女狙击手，女军人，女战斗机飞行师等等，都应该统一采购分配 . . . 保护人民，保护社会" (Chenmi 2020).
6   你是专业人士，怎么能够没有原则没有组织纪律造谣生事？
7   好像整个武汉市发展的大好局面被我一个人破坏了.
8   For example, to be admitted to a police academy, female students must score 200 points higher than their male peers. This kind of reverse affirmative action is common in many sectors. https://weibo.cn/5327831786/4399904593555850.
9   The publicizing of the discovery of COVID-19 by doctors such as Ai Fen and Li Wenliang was meaningful. I [Aviva Xue], working 800

kilometers from Wuhan, got the news via internet on January 5 and told my family and friends to avoid travelling. This was over two weeks before official acknowledgement. There must be many others who benefited from the doctors' warnings. More lives could have been saved had warnings spread earlier and more widely.

10 早知道这样，老子到处说 (Gong 2020).

11 The original posts with all the disputes were deleted by the blogger before she stopped using Weibo. Screenshots of the posts can be found in the discussion of other Weibo users, such as https://weibo.com/1502981365/J20giinp7?type=comment#_rnd1597070363021.

12 太复杂了，好像大家都有道理，把我说的没有道理了．．．一个病毒居然可以把人随时划分到某一类，然后你就有了对立方。太恐怖了！ (Qiaoluo 2020).

13 The original article has been deleted but screenshots of the news aroused discussions online: www.douban.com/group/topic/166116818/.

14 男护士具备心理承受能力更强、 情绪管控能力更强的优势.

15 一个没有怀孕、不在孕期、没有流产的女医生，当她想要作为一个正常人，争取作为劳动工作者的基本权利时，发现周围的空间已经更狭窄了，没有了。" (Debbie-Qijiang 2020).

16 The original post on Weibo has been blocked. The screenshot including the marked picture can be seen at www.douban.com/group/topic/164277716/?type=like.

17 The cartoon video can be seen online, where many viewers expressed their disgust against the morbid cartoon idols in bullet chat and comments. See www.bilibili.com/video/BV1V741177eG?from=search&seid=4211483084533568692.

18 This refers to the common practice in Chinese families that only when the first child is a girl will they have a second child, some using selective abortion to guarantee a son.

19 An official charity project, Spring Bud, claimed to be for girls only but was exposed as having embezzled donated funds to boys, including for a 19-year-old boy to buy a camera.

20 In some regions, women eat in the kitchen during family gatherings after cooking and serving the men at the table.

21 The Communist Youth League deleted the idols, and the original post with questions for Jiang Shanjiao was censored. But Chinese netizens have uploaded videos on YouTube, which requires an illegal VPN to access from China (quite common). The screen-video of the original post can be seen at www.youtube.com/watch?v=FQE7pGUwmNc.

22 你们不能靠删除存在来删除集体情绪 . . . 话语早就自动产生了话语，它和最开始我的发问没有了任何关系 . . . 无论是不是我问，都会有人问，如果你不问问题，就没有答案 (Why 2020).

23 阿中哥哥.

24 www.youtube.com/watch?v=La9jjR1Qeho.

25 https://theweek.com/articles/872717/nba-win-standoff-china. https://weibo.com/2044155203/IaU9oATSp?type=comment#_rnd1596609024987.

26 From the official website of the CPC Central Commission for Discipline Inspection (CCDI): www.ccdi.gov.cn/yaowen/202001/t20200110_207469.html.

2 Spreading feminism online

1 All ancient quotations are translated by Aviva Xue. The original Chinese version is: 大上有立德，其次有立功，其次有立言, from *Zuo Zhuan: the Twenty-fourth Year of Lord Xiang* (左传 • 襄公二十四年). www.gushiwen.org.

2 君子疾没世而名不称焉, from *The Analects: the 20th*, Wei Ling Gong (论语 • 卫灵公篇第). https://so.gushiwen.cn/guwen/bookv_46653FD803893E4F0A67CCCD1BEF2DEF.aspx.

3 老冉冉之将至兮，恐修名之不立, from *Chu Ci: Li Sao* (楚辞 • 离骚). https://so.gushiwen.cn/shiwenv_f5714bcd33e3.aspx.

4 立名者，行之极也 from *A Letter To Ren An* (报任安书). https://so.gushiwen.cn/search.aspx?value=报任安书.

5 人生自古谁无死，留取丹心照汗青 from *Across the Ling Ding Sea*. https://so.gushiwen.cn/shiwenv_5796865dca4a.aspx.

6 青史几行名姓，北邙无数荒丘 from *Xi Jiang Yue*. https://so.gushiwen.cn/shiwenv_f0033026eaec.aspx.

7 内言不出 from *Li Ji: Domestic Rules* (礼记 • 内则) (first century B.C.) https://so.gushiwen.cn/guwen/bookv_46653FD803893E4F2F8352773B 7188C9.aspx.

8 雄伟的历史是谁的历史，美的文学是谁的文学。兴亡百姓苦的百 姓到底是谁。谁在做英雄，英雄又最主要想救谁？这些"谁"的 答案可以是任何人，唯独不可以只是女人。英雄不可以只是女 人，连苦难的主体都不可以只是女人. . . 女人的苦难永远只是 小小的附带问题.

9 三星堆不是外星文明，它更有可能是母系文明.

10 The homepage of the artist on Weibo: https://weibo.com/u/7316475035

11 大道废，有仁义；智慧出，有大伪。六亲不和，有孝慈；国家昏 乱，有忠臣. The whole text, with James Legge's translation, can be read at Chinese Text Project: https://ctext.org/dao-de-jing/ens.

12 Shuang 2020; Yangxinshu 2019. https://m.weibo. cn/2429512484/4554912660984263. https://m.weibo.cn/1759932171/4346412555239087

13 商的都城殷有30平方千米，周只有3平方千米. (Daode 2021).

14 Superchat, *chao hua* (超话), can be built by any users of Weibo to discuss specific topics. In this way, people interested in a topic can better follow the relevant blogs and discuss them with one another.

15 产男则相贺，产女则杀之. From *Han Fei Zi* (韩非子 • 六反):https:// so.gushiwen.org/guwen/bookv_3539.aspx.

16 Lin Zexu (1785–1850) was a high official strongly against British merchants trading opium in China. He took actions such as destroying opium and arresting traders, which triggered the first Opium War. He was considered a nationalist hero against Western colonial invasion. It's interesting to note here his typical Confucian judgment of Zheng Yi Sao, though she defeated foreign fleets and captured Westerners on the sea.

17 These women's biographies were introduced by Weibo feminist bloggers Luomeisheng (2020) and Yeqingcheng (2021).

18 Women's labor participation keeps decreasing with increasing gender discrimination in the workplace in this century and stayed at 60.57 percent in 2019. Data from The World Bank: https://data.worldbank. org/indicator/SL.TLF.CACT.FE.ZS?locations=CN.

19 我为什么主张不加条件，一方要离就可离呢？理由是中国长期停滞在封建社会，最受压迫的是妇女，婚姻问题上妇女所受的痛苦最深...一方坚持要离就让离，主要根据广大妇女的利益提出。如加上很多条件，恰恰给有封建思想的干部一个控制和限制离婚自由的借口。过去没有这一条，发生了很多悲剧 (C. Huang 2011, 35).

20 When both sides of a couple agree to divorce, they need to take a 30-day "cooling-off" period after the first application, during which either side can withdraw it. If only one side asks for divorce, he/she must launch a lawsuit, which would be a lengthy and exhausting process. In practice, the court can also issue a cooling-off period during a divorce lawsuit, forbidding the litigants from coming to court again for a certain period of time (Luo Shuping 2017, 48–49).

21 剩女.

22 不是先有法律，才有民情的，而是先有民情，才有法律的. Lin Maomao's writings on all online platforms in mainland China are blocked. Luckily, foreseeing the censorship, some feminist netizens had compiled all her existing articles before that and now spread them through personal sharing; therefore, we cannot provide any citation information.

23 期盼一个好男人跟期盼一个好皇帝为苍生主持公道本质没什么不同.

24 他们从你那里抢走资源，然后让你拿出一部分让你拿子宫来换。羊毛出在羊身上，羊怎么可能会赢？ The feminist blogger has deleted all her posts and quitted Weibo as a result of cyber attacking in May 2021.

25 耕自己的地，你本是地主，不要去别人家里当长工.

26 父母皆祸害.

27 子女跟他们走上相同的道路，自然更加遵从他们.

28 "我并不是我，不过是我父母的儿子" and "中国人是为他儿子的缘故早就他儿子吗？"

29 坟·我们现在怎样做父亲.

30 每一个父系家庭的父都是养父，同时每一个父系家庭的母也都是养母，每一个父系家庭的孩子也都是孤儿.

31 我在家庭里是地位最低的女儿，不受重视不受关爱，然而一个孩子可以将我顶上去，我踩在孩子头上，我永远不会落底。生个孩子，那么这个孩子如同一个拯救我出苦海的救世主，她/他成了一切堕落的理由，一切痛苦的缘由，一切爱与关怀被榨取的对象，一生无悔，而且社会和法律强制她/他必须无怨无悔，不能抱怨和指责。

32 一个被窝睡不出两样人．．．他们的妈妈不爱孩子，否则不可能嫁给猪头，生这么多丑娃，丧偶育儿，内卷996.

33 首先，女性有生育权，可以决定生不生；其次，女性有继承权，可以决定爱不爱.

34 你不需要国家取消婚姻、随父姓、过年回家，你只需要自己不参与，它对你来说就是取消的.

35 对于消灭父权制这样的目标来说，对既有的价值造成冲击，并创造新的价值，不仅已经足够，而且可能是一种比任何其他手段都来得有效的变革方式.

3 Hijacking reproductive rights

1 https://so.gushiwen.org/shiwenv_f774bd9726db.aspx https://so.gushiwen.org/guwen/bookv_46653FD803893E4F6FA46D523DBC1B77.aspx.

2 https://so.gushiwen.org/guwen/bookv_46653FD803893E4F93E0729698CE6DC7.aspx.

3 产男则相贺，产女则杀之. https://so.gushiwen.cn/guwen/bookv_46653FD803893E4FDFBEAB831741BB8B.aspx.

4 因为家里没有儿子，但是其他的亲戚看着想吃绝户的比比皆是，因为他们都默认女儿是没有继承权的，我将来嫁出去了，我爸妈的财产跟我一点关系都没有 (Huoxu 2021).

5 Hou 2020. Hou Hongbin (@侯虹斌) was a very influential feminist running an account on Weibo with millions of followers and a public program on WeChat. But in April 2021, both accounts were blocked without any official explanation, so that exact citation information cannot be provided here.

6 我们要的是拓宽父权性道德、性秩序的规制范围，还是彻底推翻它？

7 The outrage of netizens is recorded as screenshots by feminist Chenzhezhe (2021).

8 禁止一切形式的代孕.

9 网络不是法外之地，为自身言行负责 。无论出于何种目的，如此炮制"代孕合法化"的谣言，着实可恶！必须予以有效治理. *China Women's News*, 2019.

10 为什么不把这条路开了，让穷男人也能多个自愿赚钱的方法呢？

11 任何人都应该破除做了"父"的执念。别再问谁谁谁不能生育该怎么办了，拥有一个孩子不是人生而就有的权利，相反创造抚养一个生命这件事首先应该是责任。当你不能生育，就不能有血缘亲子，没有人欠你一个孩子，社会不必保障每个人都必须有个孩子. Baiheihei 2019.

12 世界上最贵的红酒，要保证每一颗葡萄都来自于固定的那几株藤上，要保证每颗葡萄都经过手工挑选，要随时监控酿酒的温度。到最后那也是富人的杯中酒. Jujiuwu 2020.

13 www.governor.ny.gov/news/governor-cuomo-and-andy-cohen-rally-legalize-gestational-surrogacy-and-ban-gay-and-trans-panic.

14 这些所谓的多元平等、支持LGBT 的名人，他们的言论都被堂而皇之放在政府网站上，然后进行民意调查，这是赤裸裸的洗脑，是为吃人造势. . . 那些爱与和平，那些尊重和共情，究竟给女性群体、给孩子带来了什么？

15 一边打着我姐妹子宫的主意，一边还想我们为你们争取权利.

16 父权永不开释的囚徒.

17 主张"不跟丑人生丑孩子"的人能被仙子们随口定义为"纳粹分子"，那么搞集中营、建毒气室、做人体实验、发动 大屠杀那些人，他们又是什么？［. . .］失了智一般，满脑子就只剩下"该怎么把不喜欢的人贴上最极端最恐怖最不可饶恕的标签来讨伐他们"的念头。［而面对男人］，温情脉脉地谈共情、谈理解、谈包容的. Yingmianmian 2021a.

4 Intersectionality under the radar

1 理中客平权派站出来讲话了，女权不是特权，男女厕所都是100平米，这就是真女权；厌女派也站出来讲话了，女人就是事儿多，

麻烦人；为你好派也站出来讲话了，女人少出门，上厕所就不用
排队了；传统派也站出来讲话了，历史向来如此，你就接受现状
吧；戾气重派也站出来讲话了，你是不是受过伤，戾气这么重；太
平洋没加盖派也站出来讲话了，不满意就滚，把你送印度去，那
里连厕所都没有。还有一大派，更可气，争取女人上厕所要排队
的自由，他们的理由是，也有女人喜欢排队上厕所，排队的时
候，既可以放空自己，也可以冥想灵修，更可以打圈太极，还可
以背个单词.

2　我生来就是高山而非溪流.

3　此处的迷奸、盗摄视频外流问题一直泛滥成灾，我和小伙伴此前
就在曝光，却始终处于被压制状态，石沉大海 [. . .] 谢谢，谢
谢，谢谢。我们正在醒来，等等我们 (Guozili 2019).

4　墨西哥姐妹们，记得家务劳动罢工啊.

5　不想跟你们玩了.

6　声称要在真实基础上讨论的人，为每一条都是恶意揣测的文字摇旗
呐喊，它们在意真相吗？它们只是想要"异己"闭嘴. Xiaoshan 2020.

7　吾们试想女子何以被男子欺负，至于数千年不得翻身呢？[. . .]
女子到底有何缺陷？[. . .] 体弱乃习之使然，小脚非从古所
有，不足为生理上之根本缺陷。求根本缺陷于女子生理，便是唯
一的生育问题了. Mao, 1919/2008, p. 383.

8　为什么说女人的权利是最基础的权利？[. . .]那些看上去跟性别
毫无关系的阶级压迫能形成的根本原因在于，有性别压迫通过吃
女人形成了向上输送人吃人的链条. Huoxu 2021.

9　你能996的前提，是你回家就有食物，有干净的衣服，有舒适的
床，孩子有人带老人有人照料. . . .女性是资本主义的法宝，当
她们进入劳动力市场时，处于[. . .]同工不同酬. Chuan, 2021a.

10　原来他们都知道的，需要的时候延长时间工作，不需要的时候就
踢到一边，不用保险不用福利的非正式劳动，这种模式是一种隐
形的剥削. Chuan, 2021b.

11　如果要让一个贫困地方致富，关键之一是，找到合适的项目；关键
之二是，由女性当家作主。第二条比第一条，难一百倍、难一千
倍。那些给家里赚钱的女人，依然要挨打，依然要把钱给丈夫去找
妓女，依然看着孩子饿得嗷嗷待哺，赚再多钱，也不过是让丈夫多
喝几瓶酒罢了。男女不平等，是比一切阶层不平等更大的不平等.

12　There are many pages with mosaics from the cartoons and threats made
by anti-feminist men and JM Empire supporters. https://weibo.com/p/1
008089253fab1f1ba5b83cbb482efc7837b43.

5 The politics of feminist word-play

1 她恍然觉得不是学文学的人，而是文学本身辜负了她们. Lin 2017. The interview appeared on Readmoo, the largest e-book provider in Taiwan: https://news.readmoo.com/2017/05/05/170505-interview-with-lin-02/.

2 人类历史上最大规模的屠杀是房思琪式的强暴.

3 他硬插进来，而我为此道歉.

4 话语本能地在美女面前膨胀，像阳具一样.

5 Both terms originally refer to mushrooms commonly eaten in China. Black fungus is sometimes called "wood-ear mushroom" in Chinese-American cuisine, while needle mushrooms are suitably shaped like tiny penises.

6 According to National Bureau of Statistics for 2018: https://data.stats. gov.cn/easyquery.htm?cn=C01&zb=A030604&sj=2019.

7 从司法、文化、历史书写到日常的社会交锋，女性的弱势是极其明显的。女性就是不断被日常攻击和屠杀的一个群体。所有这些愤怒的词语跟我们的现实相比，都是软弱无力的。我根本不觉得这些词汇是个什么问题，用四平八稳的语言，能激起任何反应吗？你必须要激怒对方，要激怒这个社会的所谓"好人"，让他们看到岁月并不静好，他们是装聋作哑的帮凶. Ruobing 2021.

8 Another more insulting interpretation is that Chinese rural dog is called tian yuan quan/田园犬, therefore tian yuan nü quan/田园女权 sounds like "rural female dog."

9 The Feminist Five, activists arrested on the eve of Women's Day, 2015 for "disturbing public order" due to previous peaceful actions such as handing out flyers about sexual harassment on public transportation, are a very sensitive political topic.

10 According to the police report on surnames of newborn babies in Shanghai, one of the most international regions of China, 91.2 percent of the children born in 2018 bear the fathers' surnames: sh.people.com. cn/n2/2019/0307/c134768-32714828.html.

11 From National Bureau of Statistics: https://data.stats.gov.cn/easyquery. htm?cn=C01&zb=A030604&sj=2019.

12 https://china.unfpa.org/en/node/29358.

13 People.cn, considered to be the mouthpiece of the central government, justified the use of father's surnames in a straightforwardly misogynistic way by glorifying the passing-down of Y chromosomes: opinion.people. com.cn/n/2014/0802/c159301-25389983.html.

14 https://nytimes.com/2021/04/05/world/asia/china-uyghurs-propaganda-musical.html.

15 个体的哀伤是不能剔除的.

16 Comments have no independent URL. The webpage of the original post for the TV show is https://weibo.com/1886903325/J050ZCppK?refer_flag=1001030103_&type=comment#_rnd1588653422089.

17 当我死时，我突然开始写诗. . . 我选择被遗忘，但遗忘并不意味着原谅.

18 我的诗死去又重生在她的时纪.

Bibliography

Babiarz, K. S., Ma, P., Song, S., and Miller, G. (2019). Population sex imbalance in China before the One-Child Policy. *Demographic Research*, 40, 319–358.

Baiheihei [@白黑黑] and Shaoxi [@稍息-shaoxi]. (2019, February 9). *当我们说反婚，我们是在说些什么* [What We Talking When We Advocate Anti-Marriage].

Baiheihei [@白黑黑]. (2019, June 15). *社会秩序如何成为可能* [How Social Order Forms]. Weibo. https://m.weibo.cn/1370505990/4383301588936822.

Baiheihei [@白黑黑]. (2019, February 12). *代孕这事，女人如果还意识不到* [For Surrogacy, Women Need to Realize]. Weibo. https://m.weibo.cn/1370505990/4338861288879933.

Baobaolie [@暴暴烈甜心小鳄鱼毛毛]. (2021, February 10). *做母亲生孩子，在等国对于多数女性来说都是巨大的诱惑* [For Most Women in China, Rearing Children to Be Mother Is a Great Temptation]. Weibo. https://m.weibo.cn/6504596840/4602978792903431.

Baolie [@暴烈甜心小鳄鱼毛毛]. (2020, February 3). *火神山她力量* [Her Power on Huo Shenshan]. Weibo. https://weibo.com/5288987897/IssFu3ArI?type=comment.

Bingshuo [兵说]. (2020, February 14). *1955年授衔，谁的意见最大？并非"李云龙"，10万女兵集体退役，原因竟跟苏联有关* [Military Titles Conferring in 1955: 100,000 Female Soldiers Took off Their Uniforms]. Sohu. http://3g.k.sohu.com/t/n426144813?showType=&sf_a=weixin&from=groupmessage.

Cat With A Lighter [@拿打火机的猫]. (2020, April 27). *为什么"消费"男色并不女权* [Why "Consuming Male Bodies" Is Not Feminism] Weibo. https://weibo.com/6816655437/IFhv7zrx2?type=comment.

CCTV News [@央视新闻]. (2020, April). *致敬4万多位"火雷兄弟"* [Pay Respect to 40,000 Brothers on Leishenshan and Huoshenshan]. Weibo. https://weibo.com/tv/show/1034:4490732854247430?from=old_pc_videoshow.

Cha An [@茶 安 _2018]. (2019, August 3). 塞 壬 之 歌 [Song of Siren].
Weibo. https://weibo.com/ttarticle/p/show?
id=2309404401183199461385.

Chen, Aria. (2020, February 21). *Video of Female Medics in China Having
Their Heads Shaved Sparks Backlash Over Propaganda in the Coronavirus
Fight*. TIME. https://time.com/5788592/weibo-women-coronavirus/.

Chen, Chen. (2020, July 13). *"Stand By Her:" Chinese Feminist Rhetoric
during the COVID-19 Pandemic*. DRC: Digital Rhetoric Collaborative.
www.digitalrhetoriccollaborative.org/2020/07/13/stand-by-her-chinese-
feminist-rhetoric-during-the-covid-19-pandemic/.

Chen, H. (2021, January 23). 如果穿越见到18岁的妈妈，你会对她说什
么 [What Would You Say to Your Mom If You Met her at her Eighteen by
Time Travel]. Weibo. https://m.weibo.
cn/1792995502/4596650364118524.

Chen, J. (2016). 早期婚姻伦理文化与商代女性 [Preliminary Marriage
Ethic and Culture and Women in Shang Dynasty]. *Shandong Social
Science*, 6, 510–511.

Chengyusan [@橙雨伞微博]. (2016, August 1). 余秀华离掉包办婚姻，
为何还要给前夫精神损失费？ [Divorcing Her Husband after Forced
Marriage, Why Did Yu Xiuhua Still Need to Pay Her Ex Mental Damage
Compensation?]. Weibo. https://weibo.com/ttarticle/p/show?
id=2309404003611758728840#_0.

Chenmi [@沉迷种树的果喵]. (2020, May 20). "姐妹战疫安心行动"纪
实 [A Review of Stand By Her Project]. Weibo. https://card.weibo.com/
article/m/show/id/2309404506748722479644?_wb_client_=1.

Chenzhezhe [@陈折折]. (2021, January 18). 15 年的检日, 17 年的人日都
试水过开放代孕的风口 [Procuratorate Daily in 2015 and People's Daily
in 2017 Both Tested Water for Legalizing Surrogacy]. https://m.weibo.
cn/1851888853/4594863243531643.

China Daily. (2020, February 2). 武汉志愿者车队在行动，护送医务人员
上下班[Volunteers in Wuhan Are Taking Actions, Driving Medical
Workers to and from Work]. ChinaDaily.com. https://cn.chinadaily.com.
cn/a/202002/02/WS5e36aa6da3107bb6b579cabe.html.

China News. (2020, July 9). 全国"扫黄打非"办：快速处置所谓"国内
版N号房网站" [National Anti-pornography Office: Quickly Handle the

So-called Domestic Nth Room]. Weibo. https://m.weibo. cn/1784473157/4524725563225665

China Women's News. (2020, January 10). 坚守"春蕾计划"初衷，助 力"春蕾"成长成才[Hold Fast to the Spring Bud Project, Aiding the Growth of the Spring Bud]. Weibo. https://m.weibo.cn/ status/4459290645431751?.

China Women's News [@中国妇女报]. (2021, February 4). 中国妇女运动 的蓬勃开展，离不开这位伟大的女性 [The Thriving of Chinese Feminist Movement Is Bound with This Great Woman]. Weibo. https://m.weibo.cn/2606218210/4600975844980342.

China Women's News. (2019, December 27). 炮制"代孕合法化"的谣 言，当治 [Forging the Rumor of "Surrogacy Has Been Legalized" Will Receive Punishment]. Weibo. https://m.weibo. cn/2606218210/4454211405905960.

Chuan [@川 A1234567]. (2021a, January 10). 想解决韭菜的问题，先解决 韭菜他妈的问题 [To Settle the Problem of Labor, Settle the Problem of Labors' Mothers First]. Weibo. https://weibo.com/ttarticle/x/m/show/ id/2309404591951109292043?_wb_client_=1.

Chuan [@川 A1234567]. (2021a, January 19). 看，"后院猫" [Look, "Backyard Cats"]. Weibo. https://m.weibo.cn/status/4595016817187167?.

Chuan [@川 A1234567]. (2021b, January 19). 前几天那个代孕退货，然后 孩子没法上户口的新闻 [On the News about the Refund of Commercial Surrogacy Leading to the Child Unable to Gain Citizenship]. Weibo.

Chuan [@川 A1234567]. (2021b, January 26). 今天我对着一个经济学名词 笑了整整三分钟 [I Was Laughing Over An Economic Term for Three Minutes Today]. Weibo. https://m.weibo. cn/2606218210/4454211405905960.

Chuan [@川 A1234567]. (2021c, March 16). 前几天，看到戴锦华老师的 一个视频被截取了一段话 [Days Before, I Saw Screenscripts from a Video of Dai Jinhua with Her Words]. Weibo. https://m.weibo. cn/7513210373/4615418783990620.

ChuanA [@川 A1234567]. (2021, March 21). 三星堆是外星文明吗[Is Sanxingdui Alien Civilization]. Weibo. https://m.weibo. cn/7513210373/4617210423413035.

CJBDI. (2018). 司法大数据专题报告之离婚纠纷(2016–2017) [The Juridical Bigdata Report: Divorce Cases]. China Justice Big Data Service Platform. Beijing: CJBDI. http://data.court.gov.cn/pages/uploadDetails. html?keyword=司法大数据专题报告之离婚纠纷(2016-2017).pdf.

Claudiel [@claudiel]. (2021, January 12). 女权书单更新啦 [The Update of Feminist Reading List]. Weibo. https://m.weibo.cn/status/4592668862066856?.

cnwoman. (2021, February 08). *Evil Man*. Github: cnwoman-bot.github.io/evil-man/.

Communist Youth League. (2019, November 4). 某大V借民族苦痛历史散布性别仇恨言论 [A Poster Spread Hatred Speech Taking Advantage of the Bitter History of the Nation]. Weibo. https://m.weibo.cn/3937348351/4435055457723501.

Cui, Huiying and Yang, Kaiqi. (2020, April 15). 复盘舆论漩涡中的武汉红十字会 [Wuhan Red Cross Society in the Whirlpool of Public Criticism: A Review]. infzm. www.infzm.com/contents/181565

Czymara, C. S., Langenkamp, A., and T. Cano. (2020). "Cause for concerns: gender inequality in experiencing the COVID-19 lockdown in Germany." *European Societies*, DOI: 10.1080/14616696.2020.1808692.

Daly, Mary (1990). *Gyn/Ecology: The Metaethics of Radical Feminism*. Beacon Press.

Daode [@道德绝世小]. (2021, January 27). 所以周推翻商，到底是谁得利了 [So who benefit from Zhou dynasty's overthrowing of Shang]. Weibo. https://m.weibo.cn/2468217705/4597937218526479. https://data.stats.gov.cn/easyquery.htm?cn=C01&zb=A030604&sj=2020.

Davidson, H. (2020, September 1). Inner Mongolia protests at China's plans to bring in Mandarin-only lessons. *The Guardian*. www.theguardian.com/world/2020/sep/01/inner-mongolia-mandarin-schools-language protests-china-mandarin-schools-language.

Debbie-Qijiang [@Debbie-齐姜]. (2020, February 13). 疫情期间被某些媒体挪用的女性身体 [Female Bodies Hijacked by Some Media in the Pandemic Period]. Weibo. https://m.weibo.cn/status/4471519852359270?.

Ding, J. (1993). 毛泽东关于中国妇女解放道路的思想 [Mao Zedong's Thoughts on the Approach to Chinese Women's Emancipation]. *Journal of Chinese Women's Studies*, 04, pp. 8–12.

Dooling, Amy. *Writing Women in Modern China: The Revolutionary Years, 1936-1976*. Columbia UP.

Eagleton, T. (1996). *The Illusion of Postmodernism*. Oxford: Blackwell Publishing.

Eichner, C. J. (2014). In the Name of the Mother: Feminist Opposition to the Patronym in Nineteenth-Century France. *Signs*, 39(3), 659–683.

EleanorSforza [@EleanorSforza]. (2020, May 15). 让我难过的是 [What Makes Sad]. Weibo. https://weibo.com/3852516814/J202WjGk4?display=0&retcode=6102&type=comment.

Fang Fang. (2020). *Wuhan Diary: Dispatches from a Quarantined City*. (M. Berry, Trans.). Harper Collins Publishers.

Fengxing [@风行无叶]. (2020, March 27). 尤忒瑞斯的世界 [The World of Uterus]. Weibo. https://m.weibo.cn/status/4486973785964136?.

Ferry, Megan (2018). *Chinese Women Writers and Modern Print Culture*. Cambria.

Fiske, John. (1992). The Cultural Economy of Fandom. In Lisa A. Lewis (Ed.), *The Adoring Audience: Fan Culture and Popular Media* (pp. 30–49). Routledge.

Fortier, N. (2020). "COVID-19, gender inequality, and the responsibility of the state." *International Journal of Wellbeing*, 10(3), 77–93.

Fu, X. (2013, January 7). "川大同妻自杀案" 一审：死者家人诉讼被驳回[The First Instance of the Sucide Case of Tong Qi in Sichuan University: the Woman's Families' Appeal Rejected]. Sohu News. http://news.sohu.com/20130107/n362599824.shtml.

Geng, X. (2017, February 9). 继续严打代孕违法违规行为 [Continue To Harshly Forbid Surrogacy That Is Against Law and Regulations]. p. A03.

Gong, Jingqi. (2020, March 10). 发哨子的人：如果这些医生都能够得到及时的提醒，或许就不会有这一天 [The One Who Distributed the Whistles: If the Doctors Could Have Been Warned in Time, Today Could Be Different]. 中国医院人文建设 [China Hospital Humanitarian Construction]. www.yyrw.org.cn/e/action/ShowInfo.php?classid=5&id=2256

Guozili [@果子狸7777]. (2018, September 12). 我为你们发声？！我为你们挖坟！ [Voice for You?! I'd Rather Dig Your Grave!]. Weibo.

Guozili [@果子狸7777]. (2019, March 3). 越南75%的拐卖目的地是中国[China Is the Main Destination for Vietnamese Trafficking Victims]. Weibo. https://m.weibo.cn/6593893685/4338071405780029.

Guozili [@果子狸 7777]. (2019, May 29). China Wake Up. Weibo. https://m. weibo.cn/6593893685/4377249560154884.

Guozili [@果子狸 7777]. (2020, April 10). *纽约州强推代孕合法，一场准备已久的绞刑*[New York State Legalized Commercial Surrogacy, a Prepared Hanging of Women]. Weibo. https://m.weibo. cn/6593893685/4492212119258665.

Hangzhou Daily [@杭州日报]. (2020, May 19). *夫妻俩离婚时约定孩子随父姓女方反悔 法院判决：女方支付违约金10万* [Woman Refuses to Change Child's Surname to the Father's after Divorce: Court Rules She Must Pay 100,000 Yuan]. Weibo. https://weibo.com/1644358851/ J2FwLt1Ho?type=comment#_rnd1590374279652

Heimingdan [@黑名单]. (2021, January 12). *这 就 是 蝻 人*[This Is Men]. Weibo. https://m.weibo.cn/6873443241/4592567826778523.

Heiye [@黑夜与深海]. (2021, February 4). *前阵子微博热点反对代孕掀起热烈的讨论* [Previously Heated Debates over Surrogacy Were Seen on Weibo Hot Topics]. Weibo. https://m.weibo. cn/6500973046/4600855850136176

Hong Fincher, L. (2014). *Leftover Women: The Resurgence of Gender Inequality in China.* London & New York: Zed Books.

Hong Fincher, L. (2018). *Betraying Big Brother: The Feminist Awakening in China.* London & New York: Verso.

Hong Fincher, Leta. (2014). *Leftover Women: The Resurgence of Gender Inequality in China.* Zed Books Ltd.

Hong Fincher, Leta. (2018). *Betraying Big Brother: The Feminist Awakening in China.* Verso.

Hongli [@红鲤鲤与绿鲤鲤和驴]. (2019, November 5). *且父母之于子也，产男则相贺，产女则杀之* [People Celebrate the Birth of Sons, and Kill Newborns If They are Daughters.]. Weibo. https://m.weibo. cn/7157921721/4435409787982205.

hooks, bell. (1999). *Remembered Rapture: The Writer at Work.* Henry Holt and Company.

Huang, C. (2011). *中国婚姻调查* [Investigation of Chinese Marriage]. Beijing: The Writers Publishing House.

Huang, L. (2004). *中国女性主义* [Feminism in China]. Guangxi: Guangxi Normal University Press.

Huang, Q. (2019). The Paradox of Filial Piety in the Period of the May Fourth Movement. *Literature, History and Philosophy* (3), 24–34.

Huang, Wei. (2012). 文革时期女性形象政治化研究 [The Politicalization of Female Image during the Culture Revolution]. Shoudu Normal University, 2012.

Huo, S. (2020, November 18). *靠唱红歌、苦学，她让1800多名穷女孩考上大学，张桂梅的神话能复制吗* [By Singing Red Songs and Studying Hard, She Sent 1800 Poor Girls to Universities. Can Zhang Guimei's Myth Be Copied?]. Weibo. https://weibo.com/ttarticle/x/m/show/id/2309404572650109534726?_wb_client_=1.

Huoxu [@或许不如不见]. (2021, February 11). *继承权这个事情，凭什么女孩子不能提* [Why Can't Daughters Put Forward the Issue of Inheritance]. Weibo. https://m.weibo.cn/3524285233/4603249493279017.

Huoxu [@或许不如不见]. (2021, January 12). *为什么说女人的权利是最基础的权利* [Why We Say Women's Right is the Baseline of Human Right]. Weibo. https://m.weibo.cn/3524285233/4592489422393740.

Huoxu [@或许不如不见]. (2021, February 11). *继承权这个事情，凭什么女孩子不能提* [Why Can't Daughters Put forward the Issue of Inheritance]. Weibo. https://m.weibo.cn/3524285233/4603249493279017.

Ifeng Weekly [@凤凰周刊]. (2021, March 2). *民政部门调查55岁男子娶年轻智障女子* [The Authorities Look into the Case that 55-year-old Man Marry Young Mentally Handicapped Woman]. Weibo. https://m.weibo.cn/1267454277/4610246552586738.

Inspecting Team [@就业性别歧视监察大队]. *妇女参政论* [Women's Political Publication]. Weibo. https://weibo.com/5327831786/JtdLluhxI?type=comment#_rnd1617522987560.

Itō, Shiori. (2019). 黑箱 [*Black Box*]. (Kuang Kuang, trans.). CITIC Press Group. (Original work published 2017).

Jewkes, R., Fulu, E., Roselli, T., and Garcia-Moreno, C. (2013). Prevalence of and Factors Associated With Non-Partner Rape Perpetration: Findings from the UN Multi-country Cross-sectional Study on Men and Violence in Asia and the Pacific. *The Lancet Global Health*, 1(4), e208–e218.

Ji, Y., Wu, X., Sun, S., and He, G. (2017). Unequal Care, Unequal Work: Toward a more Comprehensive Understanding of Gender Inequality in Post-reform Urban China. *Sex Roles*, (77), 765–778.

Jiaowo [@叫我安然君]. (2020, July 29). 协和医院一护士坠楼 [A Nurse Fell to Death in Wuhan Union Hospital]. Weibo. https://weibo.com/5581654880/JdseccrJT?type=comment#_rnd1597069601190.

Jin, H. (2015, August 7). 建国以来中国生育政策的演进 [The Evolution of Reproductive Policies since the Establishment of the People's Republic of China]. Chinagate. http://cn.chinagate.cn/news/2015-08/07/content_36248175.htm.

Jinan Lives [@济南生活]. (2020, February 17). 济南向各单位倡议：延迟开学期间支持双职工家庭以女方为主在家看孩子 [Jinan Municipal Government Advised Wives in Dual-Worker Families to Apply for Staying at Home for Childcare during Delayed School Semesters]. Weibo. https://weibo.com/5329116942/IuCch7MHa?type=comment#_rnd1597072418211.

Juanmeng [@倦梦西洲的奋斗风]. (2020, May 19). 西方女性争取冠姓权的历史 [The History of Western Feminists Striving for Surname Rigt]. Weibo. https://m.weibo.cn/status/4506084079096940?.

Juanmeng [@倦梦西洲的奋斗风]. (2021a, January 18). 人口期货 [Human Futures]. Weibo. https://m.weibo.cn/7160345268/4594827599292737.

Juanmeng [@倦梦西洲的奋斗风]. (2021b, March 3). 据说子宫道德干涉生育自由 [It Is Said that Womb Morality Hinders Reproduction Right]. Weibo. https://m.weibo.cn/status/4610580403192275?.

Jujiuwu [@居酒屋的宋枣糕]. (2020, December 7). 世界上最贵的火腿 [The Most Expensive Hams in the Word]. Weibo. https://m.weibo.cn/2606218210/4454211405905960.

Junzi [@君子风寻]. (2019, September 22). 正邪不两立？ [Opposite Camps?] Weibo. https://weibo.com/ttarticle/p/show?id=2309404419301011488800.

Ke, Li. (2020, March 8). 2.8 万女性驰援湖北，占总数2/3 [28,000 Women Ride to Hubei Providing Emergency Support, Making up 2/3 of the Total]. Chang Jiang Daily-Chang Jiang Net. www.cjrbapp.cjn.cn/p/166459.html

King, Michelle (2014). *Between Birth and Death: Female Infanticide in Nineteenth-Century China.* Stanford UP.

Kong, Shuyu (2004). *Consuming Literature.* Stanford UP.

Lao Zi. *Dao De Jing.* (J. Legge, trans.). Chinese Text Project. https://ctext.org/dao-de-jing/ens

Laona [@老衲很欣慰]. (2020, May 12). 转 发 豆 瓣[Repost from Douban]. Weibo. https://m.weibo.cn/status/4503776595132507?.

Laosu [@老苏 8811]. (2020, February 5). 武汉肺炎患者求助 [Calling for Help from a Wuhan Patient]. Weibo. https://weibo.com/6350728521/IsIhe0PZm?type=comment#_rnd1597069778557.

Li, H. (2008). Family/Marriage-related Death of Women at the Beginning of Liberation. *Collection of Women's Studies* (3), 24–30.

Li, H. (2017). 性别不公：今日乡村社会观察的一个新视角 [Social Injustice: A New Perspective to Observe the Present Chinese Rural Society]. *Wuhan University Journal (Arts & Humanity)*, 70(4), 56–60.

Li, Huiying. (2019). 乡村社会治理与性别分层加剧研究 [Research on Social Governance of Rural Areas and the Increasing Disparity between Genders]. China Social Science Press.

Li, L. (2021, January 27). 代孕遭"退单"，生物学父母有义务协助落户 [The Deserted Child in Commercial Surrogacy: Biological Parents Are Obliged to Aid the Registration]. *China Women's News*, p. 006.

Li, W. (2017). "红颜祸水"论源于周人对商代的女性文化否定 [The Myth of "Beautiful Women Cause a Kingdom Collapse" Originated from the Zhou's Negation of Feminist Culture of Shang Dynasty]. *Journal of Foshan University (Social Science)*, 35(5), 18–23.

Liang, Y [@梁钰 stacey]. (2020, May 17). 中国有近四分之一的男性承认自己有过强奸行为 [Nearly ¼ Males in China Acknowledged That They Had Raped Someone]. Weibo. https://m.weibo.cn/status/4505683120709644?.

Liang, Yu [@梁钰 stacey]. (2020a, March 16). 之前"姐妹战疫安心行动"项目进展明细公示图片反复未经允许滥用的事 [About the Previous Abuse of the Publicized Items Details of Stand By Her Project without Permission]. Weibo. https://m.weibo.cn/status/4483031601294747?.

Liang, Yu. [@梁钰 stacey]. (2020b, June 24). 茶叶及其包装材料纳入了河南省疫情期间的生活物资清单，还有红头文件 [Tea Leaves and their Package Materials Were Included in the Emergency List in Pandemic Periods in Henan Province, with the Official Document]. Weibo. https://weibo.com/1306934677/J86HU1v9d?type=comment#_rnd1597067344710.

Liberty Times. (2016, October 23). 6 都同志伴侣註記1280對 男女比例懸殊高達4倍 [In 1280 Homosexual Couples Registered in Six Capitals, the

Number of Lesbian Couples Surpass Gays By 4 Times]. *Liberty Times.*
https://news.ltn.com.tw/news/life/breakingnews/1864234.

Lilian [@莉莉安说道]. (2021, February 28). "子宫道德" 听起来刺耳是
因为 [Womb Morality Is Irritating Because]. Weibo. https://m.weibo.
cn/7399215761/4609550940901059.

Lilylinmu [@Lily 林 mu]. (2020, July 30). 耕自己的地，你本是地主，不
要去别人地里当长工 [Plough your own field. You are a master; don't
work as a tenant in the field of others]. Weibo. https://m.weibo.
cn/7484401377/4532431011717444.

Lilylinmu [@Lily 林 mu]. (2021, February 13). 总有人说 "如果取消XX就
好了" [There're Always People Saying: "What if . . . Is Abolished"].
Weibo. http://m.weibo.cn/7484401377/4604163189382844.

Lilylinmu [@Lily 林 mu]. (2021a, January 18). 反对代孕 [Anti-Surrogacy].
Weibo. https://m.weibo.cn/7484401377/4594751460344176.

Lilylinmu [@Lily 林 mu]. (2021b, March 1). 这两天为啥 "子宫道德" 惹
众怒？因为她们没法道德 [Why Womb Morality Is Irritating? Because
They Have No Womb Morality]. Weibo. https://m.weibo.
cn/7484401377/4609901060686701.

Lin Maomao [@林毛毛]. (2019). 说到我孩子的德语名随父姓 [About My
Children Taking the German Surname of Their Father]. Weibo. https://
weibo.com/1671890613/HDjWw0gT7?type=comment.

Lin Yinhan. (2017, May 5). 这是关于《房思琪的初恋乐园》这部作品，
我想对读者说的事情. [This Is What I Want to Say to Readers about
Fang Siqi's First Love Paradise] [Interview]. Readmoo News. https://news.
readmoo.com/2017/05/05/170505-interview-with-lin-02/.

Lin, Yihan. (2018). 房思琪的初恋乐园 [*Fang Siqi's First Love Paradise*].
Beijing United Publishing Co., Ltd.

Liu, Huiying. (1995). 走出男权传统的樊篱：文学中男权意识的批判
[Criticism of Patriarchal Ideology in Literature]. SDX Joint Publishing
Company.

Liu, L. H., Karl, R. E., and Ko, Dorothy (Ed.). (2013). *The Birth of Chinese
Feminism: Essential Texts in Transnational Theory.* Columbia University Press.

Liu, Lydia (1995). *Translingual Practices.* Stanford UP.

LOSTINUR_ParaN [@LOSTINUR_ParaN]. (2020, February 10). 2019 年中
国大陆首播电视剧女性相关数据 [Statistics about TV Series First

Released in 2019 in Mainland China]. Weibo. https://weibo.com/5036197947/ItzJPzS0X?type=comment#_rnd1588615169395.

Lu, Chen. (2018). *Chinese Fans of Japanese and Korean Pop Culture: Nationalistic Narratives and International Fandom.* Routledge.

Luo, S. (2017). 离婚冷静期：家事审判方式改革的重大举措——评四川安岳法院签发的首份《离婚冷静期通知书》 [Calming Down Period the Vital Reform in the Judgement of Domestic Affairs: Comments on the First Calming Down Oder Issued by the Court of Anyue, Sichuan Province]. *Democracy and Legal System,* (13), 48–49.

Luomeisheng [@洛梅笙]. (2020, November 22). 王贞仪在死之前 [Before Wang Zhenyi's Death]. Weibo. https://m.weibo.cn/2034280670/4574197764331312.

Luomeisheng [@洛梅笙]. (2021, January 2). 说到中国近代以来争取将男女平等写入宪法 [Taking about Putting Women's Equal Status into the Constitute in Modern China]. Weibo. https://m.weibo.cn/2034280670/4589004895294384.

Luosheng [@我是落生]. (2020, March 10). 墨西哥姐妹们，记得家务劳动罢工啊 [Sisters from Mexico, Don't Forget to Stop Doing Housework]. Weibo. https://m.weibo.cn/5822334131/4480923636398525. https://m.weibo.cn/7513210373/4595207083153754. https://m.weibo.cn/status/4283371259723775.

Ma, Panyan [@巫山六月雪]. (2020, April 19). 我的亲身经历：旧事一 [*My Own Experiences: One*]. Weibo. https://weibo.com/ttarticle/p/show?id=2309404495564862521349#_0.

Ma, Panyan [@巫山六月雪]. (2020, April 25). 我的亲身经历：旧事五 [My Own Experiences: Five]. Weibo. https://weibo.com/ttarticle/p/show?id=2309404497542648824013#_0.

Makusishuo [@马库思说]. (2021, February 4). 姐姐，有个叫热拉的软件，是女同性恋交友软件 [Sister, There's an APP Named Rela, Which Is for Lesbians]. Weibo. https://m.weibo.cn/status/4600911307218616.

Mao, Z. (2008). 女子自立问题 [The Issue of Women's Independence]. In *The Early Articles of Mao Zedong: 1912-1920,* pp. 383–385. Changsha: Hunan People's Publishing House.

Meow [@喵小花 Meow 她妈]. (2021a, March 20). 未婚先孕，找gay假结婚 [Pregnant Unmarried and Sham Marriage with Gay]. Weibo. https://m.weibo.cn/6906810540/4616952780167655.

Meow [@喵小花 Meow 她妈]. (2021b, March 19). *未婚生孩子真的有那么难吗* [Is Being a Single Mother Really So Hard]. Weibo. https://m.weibo.cn/6906810540/4616537317315489

Mew [@Mew_.]. (2018, November 25). *边缘人的痛苦源自什么* [What's the Origin of Pain of the Maginal Groups]. Weibo. https://m.weibo.cn/status/4310178033364501?

Military Channel of China National Radio [@央广军事]. (2020, April 9). *火神山医院的护士先生* [Mr. Nurse in the Huoshenshan Hospital]. Weibo. https://weibo.com/1728148193/ICxTxCnyB?type=comment.

Morse, M. M. and G. Anderson. (2020, April 4). "The Shadow Pandemic: How The COVID-19 Crisis Is Exacerbating Gender Inequality". UN Foundation: https://unfoundation.org/blog/post/shadow-pandemic-how-covid19-crisis-exacerbating-gender-inequality/. https://mp.weixin.qq.com/s/dZ6Qpmw9ZBhPg9yqkk9ZZA

Nan, C. (2015, May 26). *李惠英：为让中央党校开设社会性别课，我蛮拼的* [Li Huiying: I strove with all my energy to introduce gender class in the Party School of Central Committee]. *China Women's News*, p. B2.

National Bureau of Statistics. (2020). *人口抽样调查-按年龄分性别比* [Population Sampling Survey: Sex-ratio by Age Groups].

Nezumi. (2017, December 29). *"父母皆祸害"小组10年考* [A Summary Study of the Team "All Parents Are the Source of Misfortune" at its Tenth Anniversary]. Douban: https://douban.com/note/651021705/.

NLGSL [@NLGSL]. (2020, March 8). *3.8 女权节* [March 8 Women's Fists Day] [Painting]. Weibo. https://weibo.com/6501758411/IxG9Pd3r2?from=page_1005056501758411_profile&wvr=6&mod=weibotime&type=comment#_rnd1590412460216.

Pande, A. (2014). *Wombs in Labor: Transnational Commercial Surrogacy in India*. New York: Columbia University Press.

Pfaelzer, Jean. (1988). The Changing of Avant Garde: The Feminist Utopia. *Science Fiction Studies*, 15(3), 282–294.

Pin Duo Duo [@拼多多]. (2021, January 11). *关于员工王某多次在某匿名社区发布"极端言论"被公司解约的情况说明* [An Notification about the Former Employee Wang Publicizing Extremist Utterances and Being Discharged by the Company]. Weibo. https://m.weibo.cn/2606218210/4454211405905960

Qiaoluo [@敲锣的我]. (2020, May 15). 太复杂了[It Was Too Complicated].
Weibo. https://weibo.com/u/3953644365?is_hot=1#_rnd1596510566322.

Qingning [@青柠甜莓]. (2021, February 13). Weibo. https://m.weibo.
cn/2833159894/4604254084662277.

Qu, C. (2021, February 12). 浙江海宁一男子大年初一杀死妻子 已被警
方控制 [A Men Killed His Wife on the First Day of the New Year and
Has Been Controlled by the Police]. *Beiqing News*. xw.qq.com/partner/
vivoscreen/20210212A05RWR00?pgv_ref=vivoscreen&ivk_
sa=1023197a.

Qunxing [@群星诗纪]. (2020, January 6). 她的诗纪 [Her Poetic Era].
Weibo. https://s.weibo.com/weibo?q=她的诗纪&Refer=user_weibo.

Ruobing [若冰]. (2021, Jan.14). 《海马星球》覃里雯：我是如何进化
为"女本位"的女权主义者[Qin Liwen and Her Planet of Sea Horse:
How Do I Evolve to a Female-centered Feminist]. The Paper. m.thepaper.
cn/baijiahao_10762445.

Saidongzhe [@赛冬者]. (2020, May). 江山娇，他们也会对你说吗？ [Jiang
Shanjiao, Do They Tell You the Same?]. Weibo. https://weibo.com/tv/sho
w/1034:4502481867046929?from=old_pc_videoshow.

Saxiaoge [@卅肖格]. (2021, February 21). 微博对我而言逐渐失去了意义
[Weibo Loses Meaning for Me]. Weibo. https://m.weibo.cn/
status/4607168210537938?.

Shangshen [@觞深之渊]. (2020, January 27). 父亲卖女为娼 [Father Sold
Daughter as Whore]. Weibo. https://m.weibo.
cn/1918121730/4597935118230483.

Shi, A. (2020, July 2). 把1600多名女孩送出大山的女校长：这才是真正
的"姐姐来了" [Female Principal Sending 1600 Girls out of the
Mountain: Sisters Are Coming]. Ifeng. https://ishare.ifeng.
com/c/s/7xmh0Otqa1S.

Shi, X. (2015, December 29). 计生法修正案为什么删除"禁止代孕"
[Why the Prohibition of Surrogacy Is Deleted from the Population and
Family Planning Law]. Ifeng. http://inews.ifeng.com/mip/46880773/
news.shtml.

Shuangla [@爽辣冷人]. (2021, January 26). 圣杯与剑2 [The Chalice and
the Blade, Video 2]. Weibo. . https://m.weibo.
cn/2429512484/4597678959232649.

Siye [@四叶重楼_貌似学霸心是渣]. (2020, July 25). 高斯定理：人造子宫 发明后会怎样 [*Gause's Law: After Man-Made Uterus*]. Weibo. https:// weibo.com/1897134231/HF7pnvsjm?type=comment#_ rnd1588642950969.

Sobotka, T. and Zhang, C. (2019). The Unexpected Rapid Normalization of the Sex Ratios at Birth in China. *2019 Annual Meeting of Population Association of America.* Austin: Population Association of America. http://paa2019.populationassociation.org/abstracts/192127.

Song, J. (2016, April 22). Wives in sham marriages hidden in the shadows. *China Daily.* www.chinadaily.com.cn/opinion/2016-04/22/ content_24759830.htm.

Souhu News. (2021, March 11). 迟到四年的生育金：上海非婚妈妈们的抗争 [Childbirth Insurance Delayed for Four Years: The Single Mothers' Struggling in Shanghai]. Weibo. https://m.weibo.cn/status/4613655688383337?.

Standbyher [@予她同行_Standbyher]. (2021, February). 姐妹战疫安心行 动项目操作手册 [Standard Operating Procedure of "Sisters Combating Pandemic" Project]. Weibo. https://weibo.com/5627318598/ K0pDV6YXo?sudaref=www.baidu.com&display=0&retcode=6102&type =comment#_rnd1625502442714.

Sun, W. (2018, September 11). 民法典同性婚姻立法修改意见操作指南 [The Guidance for Proposes on Homosexual Marriage in the Modification of the Civil Law]. Weixin. https://mp.weixin.qq.com/s?__bi z=MzI0MTE3OTk2OQ==&mid=2653301734&idx=1&sn=ac50eb9923d 6e189319b6eb592773a9d.

Taoguniang [@越南桃姑娘]. (2020, April 2). 越南姑娘去中国12年第一次 跟妈妈打电话 [Vietnamese Girl Spoke to Her Mom for the First Time after 12 Years' Separation]. Weibo. https://m.weibo. cn/7480950994/4621635199700111.

Tenggeli News [腾格里新闻]. (2020, September 4). "五个不变"如何落 地 自治区教育厅权威回应[How to Guarantee the "Five Not to Change," the Authoritative Response from the Educational Bureau of the Autonomous Region]. Weibo. https://m.thepaper.cn/newsDetail_ forward_9042089.

The Paper News. (2020, June 29). 17 岁少女举报被爸妈逼婚嫁给邻村男 子，错过上高中 [A Seventeen-year Old Girl Reported Her Parents

Forcing Her to Get Married out of High School]. Weibo. https://weibo. com/ttarticle/x/m/show/id/2309354521133759136000?_wb_client_=1.

The People's Daily. (2019, November 27). 你怎么看家暴只有0次和无数次 [Domestic Violence Never Happens Just Once]. Weibo. https://weibo. com/2803301701/Ii6QSzvv6?type=comment.

Tianyancha [@天眼查]. (2019, September 2). *Blued 计划赴美上市* [Blued Plans to Enter the Share Market in the US]. Weibo. https://m.weibo.cn/ status/4412087214191008?.

Tianyancha [@天眼查]. (2020, January 19). *代孕产业再被曝光，关联公 司股价却大涨*[While Surrogacy Service Is Exposed, the Share Price of the Related Company Is Rising Dramatically]. Weibo. https://m.weibo. cn/status/4595160212842829.

Ueno, C. (1990/2020). *Patriarchal System of Capitalism.* (Y. Zou, and M. Xue, Trans.) Hang Zhou: Zhejiang University Press.

UN Women. (2020). *The First 100 Days of the COVID-19 Outbreak in Asia and the Pacific: A Gender Lens.* www2.unwomen.org/-/media/field%20 office%20eseasia/docs/publications/2020/04/ap_first_100-days_covid-19-r02.pdf?la=en&vs=3400.

Voiceyaya. (2020, January 3). *顺便说一句* [By the Way]. Weibo. https://m. weibo.cn/status/4589199414002329?

Voiceyaya. (2020, October 28). *别在那感动自我了* [Don't Indulge in Self-empathy]. Weibo. https://m.weibo.cn/1542701343/4565027090333963.

Wang, C. (2015, 12 24). *代孕问题不宜随修法"搭车"解决* [The Issue of Surrogacy Is Not Suitable To Be Settled Incidentally with the Change of Law]. *China Women's News*, p. A01.

Wang, J. (2017, February 3). *生不出二孩真烦恼* [It Bothers People Not Being Able to Rear the Second Child]. *The People's Daily*, p. 019.

Wang, K. (2019). "Ching I Sao in Fact and Fiction." *Comparative Literature and Transcultural Studies*, 3(1), 82–95.

Wang, L. (2021, March 4). *以下是在豆瓣鹅组里看到的评论* [Here Are Some Comments Found from Douban]. Weibo. https://m.weibo. cn/2602485724/4610844706472647.

Wang, Q. (2018). From "Non-governmental Organizing" to "Outer-system"— Feminism and Feminist Resistance in Post-2000 China. *Nora—Nordic Journal of Feminist and Gender Research*, 26(4), 260–277.

Wang, S. (2020). 王阳明六经 "删述" 说发微——兼论文化生态的净化 [Historical Probe of WANG Yangming's Ethical Explanation of Confucian Deletion and Compilation of Six Classics from Perspective of Purification of Cultural Eco-system]. *Journal of Hubei University (Philosophy and Social Science)*, 47(5), 85–93.

Wang, Z. (1999). *Women in the Chinese Enlightenment: Oral and Textual Histories.* University of California Press.

Wangtaixu [@王太虚 wray]. (2021, January 10). 因为看到同事被抬上救护车我被拼多多开除了 [I Was Fired by Pin Duo Duo For Witnessing My Colleage Carried to An Ambulance]. Weibo. https://m.weibo.cn/1544481381/4591917712809183. Weibo. https://m.weibo.cn/1370505990/4337805569873608.

Wesoky, S. R. (2016). Politics at the Local-Global Intersection: Meanings of Bentuhua and Transnational feminism in China. *Asian Studies Review*, 40(1), 53–69.

Wesoky, S. R. (2016). Politics at the Local-Global Intersection: Meanings of Bentuhua and Transnational feminism in China. *Asian Studies Review*, 40(1), 53–69.

White, Hayden. (1973). *Metahistory: The Historical Imagination in Nineteen Century Europe.* The Jones Hopkins University Press.

Why It Goes On Forever [@为什么它永无止境]. (2020, February 18). 这事真的火得莫名其妙，删得也莫名其妙 [It Arose Suddenly and Was Deleted Suddenly]. Weibo. https://weibo.com/3102117384/IuKrTgCp3?type=comment.

Wittig, Monique. (1992). *The Straight Mind and Other Essays.* Beacon Press.

World Economic Forum. (2021, March 30). *Global Gender Gap Report, 2021.* www.weforum.org/reports/global-gender-gap-report-2021.

Wuhan Daily. (2020, February 12). 流产10天后，武汉90后女护士重回一线 [Ten Days after Miscarriage, the Young Nurse Returned to Her Position on the Frontline]. Guancha. www.guancha.cn/politics/2020_02_12_535828.shtml.

Wuhou [@午后的水妖]. (2020, March 3). 打着婚姻旗号的人口买卖 [Population Trafficking in the Name of Marrigae]. Weibo. https://m.weibo.cn/2606218210/4454211405905960.

Wuming [@物鸣的垃圾箱]. (2021, February 14). 女人与家国情怀 [Women and National Emotional Bound]. Weibo. m.weibo. cn/1111790250/4604496422111719.

Wuren [@写百合的无人]. (2021, February 2). 街头格斗知识科普 [Some Combat Skills Used in Actual Fighting]. Weibo. https://m.weibo. cn/5191030913/4600280488347218. www.scmp.com/news/people-culture/china-personalities/article/3118364/chinese-actress-zheng-shuangs-surrogacy.

Wyujia [@W瑜伽无人认领]. (2020, November 5). 突然账号异常 [My Account Turned Abnormal Suddenly]. Weibo. https://m.weibo. cn/1800751037/4545802607002992.

Xiao, X. and Wu W. (2010). 三星堆遗址仁胜村土坑墓出土玉石器初步研 究 [A Preliminary Study of Jade and Stone Items from Tombs of Rensheng Village in Sanxingdui Site]. Sichuan Cultural Relics, 2, 33–43.

Xiaoshan [@小珊 liang3]. (2020, October 18). 一个女人开口说话的代价 [The Cost for A Woman Speaking Aloud]. Weibo. https://m.weibo. cn/7229051325/4561485772885365.

Xiaoxiang Morning News. 全国扫黄打非办：淫秽漫画作者JM被拘留 [The National Anti-pornography Office: the Author of Pornographic Cartoon Is Arrested]. Baijiahao. https://baijiahao.baidu. com/s?id=1686862429771605397&wfr=spider&for=pc.

Xie, B. H. (2021, 2 2). 街头格斗知识科普.

Xie, Lei. (2020, February 17). 疫情下的武汉咖啡馆：就算店垮了，最后 一杯咖啡也给医生 [Wuhan Cafe in Pandemic: Even if the Cafe Goes Bankrupt, the Last Cup Would Be Offered to the Doctors]. The Beijing News. www.bjnews.com.cn/inside/2020/02/17/ 690861.html.

Xinhua News Agency. (2019, February 19). 中共中央国务院关于坚持农业 农村优先发展做好"三农"工作的若干意见 [Some Ideas on Inciting the Prior Development of Agriculture and Rural Areas for the Accomplishment of Work in Agriculture, Rural Areas and Rural Dwellers from Central Commmission of Communist Party, China and the State Council]. Government of China: www.gov.cn/zhengce/2019-.02/19/ content_5366917.htm.

Xu, Ruijuan. (2014). 永宁摩梭"母系"文化词群研究 [Matrilineal Language and Culture of Mosuo People of Yong Ning County]. The Ethnic Publishing House.

Xunxunzi [@-寻-寻-子-]. (2021, January 17). 之前一直以为我国女性是有完整的堕胎权的 [Before, I Thought Chinese Women Enjoyed Complete Abortion Right]. Weibo. https://m.weibo.cn/status/4594432949881750?.

Yang, Y., and Yang, H. (2021, 1 21). 郑爽的"大瓜"并不是"娱闻" [Zhengshuang's Scandal Is Not Only an Entertainment]. *China Women's News*, 004.

Yangguang [@阳光阳光闪闪亮]. (2021, February 10). 计划生育 [Childbirth Plan]. Weibo. https://m.weibo.cn/status/4603005275481853?.

Yangxinshu [@yangxinshu]. (2019, March 5). 母缘断裂 [The Breaking-up of Mother-Child Bound]. Weibo. https://m.weibo.cn/1759932171/4346427037235054.

Yeqingcheng [@作家叶倾城]. 中国第一代女留学生中 [Among the First Generation of Chinese Females Studying Abroad]. Weibo. https://m.weibo.cn/1182419985/4619691731456544.

Yili [@伊丽莎白骨精啊]. (2021, February 28). 一大早上就给我震撼到了 [I Was Shocked This Morning]. Weibo. https://m.weibo.cn/status/4609493851179506?.

Yingmianmian [@硬晚晚]. (2020, Decmber 7). 其实婚姻的机制很简单[The Mechanism of Marriage Is Quite Simple]. Weibo. https://m.weibo.cn/6512113818/4579587667272013.

Yingmianmian [@硬晚晚]. (2020, November 2). 我非常反感 [I Dislike It]. Weibo. https://m.weibo.cn/6512113818/4566849620288140.

Yingmianmian [@硬晚晚]. (2021, February 21). 真是大水冲了龙王庙的好戏 [Such A Great Drama]. Weibo. https://m.weibo.cn/6512113818/4607141618651068.

Yingmianmian [@硬晚晚]. (2021a, February 26). 其实我对首页一些人开始自嘲"纳粹"这件事感到特别哭笑不得 [I Don't Know How to React to Some Feminists Reacting to the Accusation by Embracing the Name of Nazis]. Weibo. https://m.weibo.cn/6512113818/4608862244572038.

Yoon, S.-Y. (2020, March 29). "Nth Room": A Digital Prison of Sexual Slavery. Korean Joongang Daily. https://koreajoongangdaily.joins.com/2020/03/29/features/DEBRIEFING-Nth-room-A-digital-prison-of-sexual-slavery/3075441.html.

Yu, Xiuhua. (2020, April 13). 爱国贼和爱国奴：关于方方日记的一点小想法 [Traitors and Slaves in Name of Patriots: Some Thoughts on Fang Fang's Diary]. Weixin.

Zhang, H. (2021, February 26). 商业代孕入刑：保障生命尊严杜绝生育权滥用 [Adding Commercial Surrogcy into the Penal Code: Guarantee the Dignity of Life and Prohibit the Misuse of Reproductive Right]. *China Women's News*, p. 006.

Zhang, P. (2019, June 10). ChinaWakeUp a call to action as women expose Twitter accounts selling date-rape drugs, porn. The Star. www.thestar.com.my/tech/tech-news/2019/06/10/chinawakeup-a-call-to-action-as-women-expose-twitter-accounts-selling-daterape-drugs-porn.

Zhang, P. (2021, January 20). Chinese actress Zheng Shuang's surrogacy scandal rocks social media, prompting fresh debate over China's ban of the practice. *South China Morning Post*.

Zhao, C., and Fan, L. (2020). 论婚姻与生育的社会属性——少子化背景下浙北乡村婚育模式嬗变的田野观察 [On the Reproductive and Sociological Meaning of Marriage: A Field Study on the Evolution of Marriage Pattern in Northern Zhejiang Province against Low Birth Rate]. *Hebei Academic Journal*, 40 (4), 198–205.

Zhao, M. (2018). 孔子"删诗"说的来源与产生背景 [The Origin and Background of the Sayings of "Confucius Delecting Poems"]. *Confucius Studies*, 5, 22–30.

Zhou, D. and Guo Y. (2013). "Gender, Power and Identity Construction – Taking Dazhai's "Iron Girls" as a Case." *Nationalities Research in Qinghai*, 24(1), 5–10.

Zhou, D. and Guo Y. (2013). "Gender, Power and Identity Construction – Taking Dazhai's "Iron Girls" as a Case." *Nationalities Research in Qinghai*, 24(1), 5–10.

Zhou, X. (2021, February 28). 如果你还是觉得"子宫道德"这个说法有攻击性 [If You Still Feel Womb Morality Aggressive]. Weibo. https://m.weibo.cn/2501511785/4609550131658953.

Zijingshu [@紫荆树]. (2020, February 15). 怀孕9个月护士不顾家人反
    对，奔赴在抗疫一线 [Nurse with Nine-Month Pregnancy Working on
    the Frontline of Coronavirus Response, Regardless of the Opposition
    from Families]. Weibo. https://weibo.com/1198220993/
    IuhnDzOt0?type=comment#_rnd1597071724587.
Zuo, C. and Yang W. (2017). "殷周革命"中女性贵族等级身份的变迁
    [Changing Status in the Hierarchal Society of Aristocratic Women
    during Zhou Replacing Shang]. *Ningxia Social Science*, 1, 191–196.

Index